Herrick Johnson

Christianity's Challenge

Herrick Johnson

Christianity's Challenge

ISBN/EAN: 9783744662697

Printed in Europe, USA, Canada, Australia, Japan

Cover: Foto ©Lupo / pixelio.de

More available books at **www.hansebooks.com**

Christianity's Challenge;

AND

SOME PHASES OF CHRISTIANITY,

SUBMITTED

FOR CANDID CONSIDERATION.

BY

THE REV. HERRICK JOHNSON, D.D.

CHICAGO:

CUSHING, THOMAS & COMPANY.

1881.

57476

CONTENTS.

		PAGE.
I.	CHRISTIANITY'S CHALLENGE,	9
II.	CHRISTIANITY'S BOOK,	27
III.	CHRISTIANITY'S CHRIST,	61
IV.	CHRISTIANITY A GOSPEL OF DEFINITENESS,	89
V.	CHRISTIANITY'S VIEW OF MAN,	117
VI.	CHRISTIANITY NOT A FAILURE,	139
VII.	CHRISTIANITY AND ENDLESS DEATH,	165
VIII.	CHRISTIANITY AND ENDLESS LIFE,	189
IX.	CHRISTIANITY AND PLEASURE,	211
X.	CHRISTIANITY AND BUSINESS,	235
XI.	CHRISTIANITY AND WOMAN,	253

NOTE.

———

This volume comprises the Sunday afternoon lectures delivered during the past winter in Farwell Hall, Chicago, under the auspices of the Young Men's Christian Association, together with several new and hitherto unpublished papers upon vital themes. They are now given to the public in response to urgent demands, and with the full conviction that they are calculated to have a marked and beneficial effect upon the religious thought of the times.

The Publishers.

Chicago, April 15, 1881,

PREFACE.

The popular doubt of the day is chiefly born of popular assaults on Christianity. The great bulk of the prevailing skepticism is unscientific. Dashing, audacious attacks on minor details of the Christian system have caught the ear of the public; and the very elaborateness of the defence has so magnified these details, as to lift them to undeserved conspicuity. Insectivorous critics may thrust a few seeming flaws in any work to such prominence, and answers to these critics may so keep these seeming flaws in the public eye, that all the glories of the great work will be missed in a consideration of trifles.

Christianity can afford to take the aggressive, to compel a hearing, to challenge popular doubt to look some of Christianity's more important phases honestly in the face. Here are its "Book" and its "Christ." Here are its definite doctrines, and its views of man, matching marvelously the facts. Here are its successes, challenging, in anything like the same conditions, an approach to comparison. These things, and things like them, are to the last degree evidential. Their exhibition is their demonstration. They are Christianity's setting, environment, substance, achievement. They are the ever increasing marvels and the ever brightening glories of the gospel. Instead of a bout with the infidel merry-makers at points where they choose to attack, let prevalent scepticism be pressed with the business of accounting for these transcendent forces and facts.

It was with this design in part, that these lectures were first delivered. They were meant, however, to serve other and immediately practical purposes. That they may prove steps into the kingdom of truth for some, and helps to a surer footing in the King's highway for others, is the hope with which they are now given to a wider public.

THE AUTHOR.

I.

CHRISTIANITY'S CHALLENGE.

Which of you convinceth me of sin?—CHRIST.

Though all the winds of doctrine were let loose to play upon the earth, so truth be in the field we do injuriously, by licensing and prohibiting, to misdoubt her strength.—MILTON.

> Truth is large. Our aspiration
>   Scarce embraces half we be;
> Shame to stand in his Creation
>   And doubt Truth's sufficiency.
> To think God's song unexcelling
> The poor tales of our own telling.
> —MRS. E. B. BROWNING.

Prove all things: hold fast that which is good.—PAUL.

CHRISTIANITY'S CHALLENGE.

Truth of any kind is not harmed by investigation. Truth is not afraid of investigation. If it be truth that nearly concerns us, it demands investigation—has a right to it. We have no right to ignore it, or to treat it with indifference.

Now Christianity asserts itself to be the most vital truth pertaining to man. Its founder wrapped all truth up in His own personality, and boldly said, "I am the Truth." But such sweeping claim as this is not addressed to an unthinking, unreasoning credulity. Along with its matchless assertion Christianity presses its fearless challenge: "Which of you convinceth me of sin?" Its own demand is that it shall be put to the proof. It is the friend—the steadfast, changeless friend—of free inquiry. It is not afraid of the light. It addresses men as rational creatures, bound to act rationally. It appeals to men as moral agents, capable of acting in view of moral motives. It

9

asks no blind faith. It stands upon its reason. It appeals to the law and the testimony. It speaks as to wise men and bids them judge calmly, intelligently, searchingly, but honestly, what it says. It asks no favors because it deals with sacred things; but neither is it on this account to be approached with prejudice.

Here are some of the words with which it addresses men: "Come now and let us reason together." "Is Satan divided against himself?" "Doth a devil cast out devils?" "Which of you convinceth me of sin?" "And if I say the truth, why do ye not believe me?" "Try the spirits, whether they be of God." "Prove all things; hold fast that which is good." It is in just this way that Christianity has always fearlessly flung out its challenge, and demanded investigation. ·

It has met with widely different treatment. Some have given it no heed whatever. Some, with no honest consideration of its claims, have laughed it to scorn. Some have so violently opposed it and made such an uproar about it, that its preachers have been obliged to flee for personal safety. Some have listened attentively and respectfully to a statement of its claims—have examined the records, consulted the evidences, searched the Scriptures and honestly tried to know what they had to say and whether its sayings were worth heeding.

Which is the wise and manly thing to do? Here is a cause that now for ages has been a potent factor in the world's life. It has done some revolutionary things. It has turned the world upside down. Something is in it, therefore. It is not to be tossed off with a sneer. It deserves at least a thoughtful attention. Surely it is rational to examine this matter. Surely it is worth every man's while to see whether these things of which Christianity speaks, are so. Come ye doubters, skeptics, half-believers, unbelievers, unsettled as to your convictions, in doubtful attitude, or neutral attitude, or hostile attitude—come, accept Christianity's challenge. Look its claims squarely in the face, and prove it to be false, or believe on its Lord. Let me name some of the grounds of its challenge, and the reasons why it is worth your thoughtful consideration.

1. Christianity is a conspicuous and widely influential fact in the world. For eighteen centuries it has had growing place and power among men. There are certain historical data in connection with it that are not now, and that doubtless never will be called in question. They are put beyond the legitimate application of the most destructive

criticism. They have been recognized and acknowledged by the most learned opponents of the Christian system. They are established by all that amount and variety of evidence by which anything in the past is made worthy of belief. They have entered into the actual life of the best races of people. They have shaped the development and directed the currents of history. It is impossible to explain the history of the world without admitting the reality of these facts. They are just as much a part of the past as the death of Cæsar, or the propagation of Mohammedanism, or the conquest of William the Norman, or the career of Napoleon.

No one intelligently questions that Jesus was a historical person, who lived and died in Palestine about eighteen and a half centuries ago. The fact of His death, and the singular manner of His death, are as clearly established as the fact and the manner of any other death in the distant past. Such a man as Jesus of Nazareth really appeared on earth about the time the four gospels fix. Those four gospels contain, in substance, the history of His life. This is conceded by all who, at this day, on the ground of scholarship and intellectual competency, are entitled to consideration. The miraculous may be denied—is denied. Strauss denied it. He

charged that it was thrust into the record and associated with Jesus as myths or legendary tales, that
"grew up out of the story-telling or marveling
habit of the early disciples." But Strauss did not
deny that Jesus once lived, and that He was the
founder of Christianity. Theodore Parker denied
that Jesus was God, and denied the supernatural
in connection with Jesus' life and character, but
Theodore Parker said, "Shall we be told such a
man never lived; that the whole story is a lie?
Suppose that Plato and Newton never lived. But
who did their wonders and thought their thoughts?
It takes a Newton to forge a Newton. What man
could have fabricated Jesus? None but Jesus."
Renan denied the supernatural in the recorded life
of Jesus; but Renan said, "Whatever may be the
surprises of the future, Jesus will never be surpassed. He founded the pure worship of no age,
of no clime, which shall be that of all lofty souls to
the end of time,"

Christianity is no fiction, therefore; no dream of
an enthusiast, no mere conjecture, no concocted
fable, but a fact, a palpable, undeniable fact, and a
fact of a very extraordinary kind. Its history lies
imbedded in the history of the world's intelligent
and ruling nations. The history of civilization
cannot be written without writing the history of

Christianity. Take one point by way of illustration. Christianity's birth gave the world a new departure, and history a new date—A. D. (*Anno Domini*), the year of the Lórd. What is that, appearing in all our dates and superscriptions, but the assent of the leading civilizations to the fact that with Christianity came a new era, whose beginning and progress should be forever inseparable from Christianity itself. Of course, there have been, and there are, other facts than this of Christianity. Mohammedanism is a fact. Buddhism is a fact. Confucianism is a fact. Perpetuated, too, these are, and influential; but only over stagnant and dead peoples. They are not aggressive facts. They do not welcome light and cannot bear it. They do not and they cannot push themselves and win place and power in this high noon of nineteenth-century intelligence, and amidst the best thought of our time. Christianity not only does this, but does more. It boldly grapples with these huge hulks of superstition—these perpetuated and hoary systems of religion, and is shaking them to pieces, winning their adherent races to its own ideas. It is thus gradually displacing these dead facts, having a show of perpetuity, by the greater and living fact—by itself!

2. But, secondly, Christianity claims to be a

divine fact. It avows itself to be from God—his
last message to men. Its calm and confident assertion is as to its doctrine, its law, its kingdom, its
life, its founders, that they are divine. It boldly
challenges investigation and demands belief on
this very ground. "Which of you convinceth me
of sin ?" asks Jesus. "If my words are not the
words of God, and if my works are not the works
of God, then the charge of imposture is true, and
I am guilty of blasphemy. But who of you convinceth me of this sin? I challenge the proof."
Here is the present sphere of skepticism. Here is
the battle of the evidences. Is the Christian religion from God any more than any other of the
prevalent religions is from God? Was this Jesus
of Nazareth a real worker of miracles? Did He
rise from the dead? Christianity is a historical
fact. Is it a supernatural fact? Scepticism no
longer says, "There is no God!" Science now
joins with Scripture in leaving that bold, arrogant,
monstrous assertion to "the fool." We have gotten
away from open and avowed atheism. Blank and
utter denial of God's existence is too much for
modern doubt. Agnosticism, the latest, and, at
present, most popular form of unbelief, says,
" There may be a God; but we cannot know that
there is." Well, Jesus talks as if He knew. The

four gospels read as if there were no room for
doubt.   Through and through the New Testament
and the Old Testament is the *claim* that God is
there speaking to men.   And the Christ of the
gospels, the Christ of Christianity, is represented as
God manifest in the flesh.   This person, this God-
man called Jesus, asserts over and over His divine
character and His divine mission.   He claims divine
authority, assumes divine prerogatives, professes to
be the giver of divine life, and declares that the
destinies of men forever depend on the reception
or rejection of Him and His truth.   The system of
truth He founded, and of which He Himself is the
center and soul, is called the Christian system, or
the Christian religion—Christianity.   It stands
professedly as God's message to man.

Friends, this may be the literal truth.   It may
be that every thing claimed by Christianity is well
founded; that God does here speak authoritatively
and finally to men.   If true, it certainly is worth
your while, and that of every living being, to hear
and heed what God has to say.   Is Christianity
true?   Have you made up your mind as to that?
What is your mind?   Is it utterly skeptical?   If so,
on what ground?   Have you accepted Christianity's challenge, and instituted inquiry, and honestly
looked the matter all over, so that you have not

guesses, nor wishes, nor notions, but intelligent, positive convictions? That would be the manly thing. That ought to be the only thing. Is that the thing you have done? If not, don't you think the skepticism somewhat contemptible?

But perhaps you are not utterly skeptical. You have heard, however, a great deal that is suggestive of doubt as to some things in Scripture. You have heard of men making merry with the so-called "Mistakes of Moses." You have heard some very remarkable statements about the gospels. You have heard the old, clear, definite, positive doctrines of Scripture set aside, and a gospel of indefiniteness heralded as the gospel for our time, of which Far-rar, with his "Eternal Hope," Matthew Arnold, with his "Sweetness and Light," and Henry Ward Beecher, with his exegesis by imagination, are the chief apostles. You have heard more or less of this and much else that is afloat in public prints and in the talk of the street, and doubts are lodged in your mind. You find yourself questioning some things— wondering if, after all, they are true. You still yield a general assent to Christianity, but it is some-what vague and indefinite. Uncertainties have taken the place of confidences as regards many so-called biblical truths. Down in your secret heart it is beginning to be doubtful whether, after all, the

2

things contained in the gospel, all of them, as from God, are really so. Take for example your thought about God, about yourself, about the future. Now Christianity *claims* that as to *all* its revelation, as to every doctrine of it, every disclosure of the divine character, every unfolding of human destiny, every promise and every penalty, every offer of everlasting reward and every declaration of everlasting punishment, it is from God. And surely, if God has spoken here, no creature of God should be satisfied with doubts or uncertainties. You ought not to be taking notions for statements, guesses for facts, wishes for arguments, and the kind of God you want for the kind of God He is. It is a matter of infinite moment. Christianity claims to be divine in all its revelation of God, of man, of sin, of duty, of destiny.

Other facts, I know, make the same claim. But they do not come to the light to have their claims sifted. Christianity does. Other religions claim to be from God. But many of them are so associated with immorality and lust, and bear such shameful and ungodly fruit, as to carry the evidence of their falsity on their face. All of them fall in with sinful nature, and flow with the current, and have no out-reaching, aggressive, uplifting vitality. They breast and turn back no tides of evil. As

CHRISTIANITY'S CHALLENGE. 19

their adherent races rot and die, they too rot and die, and in their stagnant pools to-day they are going through the different stages of decay and dissolution. Christianity meets men with some show of reason in its divine claim; for it is constantly rising and raising its adherent races with it. Something is in it, therefore, something possesses it, separating it utterly from everything else in this world. That something, it says, is God! Christ says that He is the truth, that the truth is the word, that the word is God. Is this false? Then to the law and the testimony. Listen to the challenge: "Which of you convinceth Me of sin?" Is the claim true? Listen again: "Why do ye not believe Me?" Surely it is the part of reason instantly to see whether these things are so, and honestly and earnestly to act upon them if they are.

3. But thirdly, Christianity claims to be of vast personal concern to every living being. Of course a revelation from God would be of some moment, in any event. But it might be to only a part of the human family; and it might be only preliminary and of subordinate importance compared with other possible revelations. Christianity, however, claims to be of infinite moment, and to each man it declares itself to be of equal consequence. Christianity asserts itself to be a finality. This is its own state-

ment. Nothing is to come after. What it settles, in the relations of men to God, will be eternally settled. It claims to be God's last message. It foretells no other revelation—forbids the reception of any other—sweeps the entire future with its everlasting settlements of reward or punishment and comes burdened only with its own struggles and its own millennial glories. Its one great promise is eternal life through Jesus Christ to them that believe. Its one great revelation of punishment is the final and remediless doom of those who believe not. The earliest theophanies were only preludes to Judaism; and Judaism itself was only a preparation for Christianity. But if Christianity be true, it is the last thing. God has nothing else with which to affect men and change their condition. This fixes destinies eternally. According to its own words, he that believeth it shall be saved. He that believeth it not shall be damned. From the judgment seat of its divine founder, the wicked shall go away into everlasting punishment—the righteous into life eternal.

And these transcendent interests and final settlements are claimed by Christianity to have relation to every individual soul. The personality of this message from God and the universality of it are alike unmistakable. All are gone out of the way,

all need the redemption of Christ, all must repent,
all must die, all must stand before the judgment
seat, every one must give account of himself to
God, and every one shall there receive the things
done in his body, according to that he hath done,
whether it be good or bad. There is no discharge
in that war. There is no escape from that tribunal.
God shall bring every work into judgment with
every secret thing. And there is no name under
heaven whereby men, any man, can escape the
condemnation of that court of last resort and be
saved, but the name of Jesus. These are the
claims and doctrines of Christianity. These are the
revelations of Him who assumed to be God manifest in the flesh, and to come into the world that
the world through Him might be saved. And I
ask if they do not magnify and make clear to every
mind the unutterable folly of dismissing Christianity, or doubting it, without an honest and
thorough consideration. If such consequences, so
personal to each and so fearful and remediless, are
declared to hang on the practical denial or admis-
sion of the claims of the gospel, then nothing
whatever ought so soon to be settled in the case of
every living soul as whether these claims are true
or false. Come, then, and let us reason together.
If you have a doubt about Christianity or any of

its claims—if you are rejecting any truth concerning the divine character, or vour own character, or the awards of the judgment, or the eternal future, claimed here to be the truth of God, without ever having fully and finally made up your mind whether the claim is well founded (and you may be doing this while even a member of the church) .in the name of the Christianity I preach and of the Christ in whose stead I stand before you, I demand that you stop—stop now, in the midst of whatever may be absorbing your attention or engaging your thought; stop and settle this question once for all. Dare to face it—to give it instant and earnest heed. You may have thought of it before. But you have not so sincerely and so thoroughly given it consideration that you stand with reference to it as one whose mind is made up. It is worth such consideration. It ought to have it—ought to have it now. Christianity is everything to you, or it is nothing. It is of inconceivable consequence, or it is as worthless and as wicked an imposition as was ever brought before the world.

Many of you, doubtless, are going on, yielding a kind of general assent to Christianity's divine claims, but exhibiting, nevertheless, a practical infidelity. You are not so certain about these things after all. You find yourselves possibly cherishing a sort of half-defined hope that your case is not so bad, and that, even without a personal interest in the Christian religion, it will not go so wholly ill with you as some zealous preachers of Christianity would make out. Well, is it not time that this whole question was put at rest? Is it not worth your while to settle decisively your belief in, and your relation to, a fact so conspicuous and influential in the world, coming with such awful claims of authority, and making such demands upon you, and whose acceptance or rejection involves such fearful consequences, *if true ?* Is it right, is it manly, is it well, is it wise, to dismiss this matter with an "Oh, I guess there's some doubt about these things?" Guess! Should a man be guessing on eternity?

Christianity, Christ, heaven, hell, the judgment, sin, holiness, God—these, and whether they be true or false, and our personal relations to them, whether they be right or wrong, are things *to know about*, not to be *doubting* or *guessing* about. Why not determine, every one of you unsettled in regard to your personal relation to this gospel of Jesus Christ, to begin this very hour, seriously and thoughtfully, with an open Bible and a teachable spirit, to see once for all whether these things are so, and to settle once for all what you will do with

Christianity's claims. What it is in the world to-day, and what it assumes in its address to your consciences and hearts, make it above all things else in the universe worth your instant and thoughtful attention. Give it that, and resolve that you will not be swerved from giving it that, till you are put past all doubt as to where you exactly stand and as to what you exactly believe with reference to this so-called gospel of God, and I am persuaded you will be found accepting ere long with an adoring and grateful heart its proffered terms of mercy.

II.

CHRISTIANITY'S BOOK.

Revelation is not a vain thing for us. It is our life. —WESTCOTT.

One gem from that ocean is worth all the pebbles from earthly streams.—McCHEYNE.

> Every hour
> I read you, kills a sin,
> Or lets a virtue in
> To fight against it.—ISAAK WALTON.

The law of the Lord is perfect, converting the soul. The testimony of the Lord is sure, making wise the simple. The statutes of the Lord are right, rejoicing the heart. The commandment of the Lord is pure, enlightening the eyes. The judgments of the Lord are true and righteous altogether. More to be desired are they than gold, yea, than much fine gold; sweeter also than honey and the honey-comb. Moreover, by them is thy servant warned; and in keeping of them there is great reward.

—THE PSALMIST.

CHRISTIANITY'S BOOK.

"And beginning at Moses and all the Prophets, He expounded unto them in all the Scriptures the things concerning Himself." Here is Christ, the recognized founder of Christianity, going through the Old Testament Scriptures to show that they are filled with "things concerning Himself."

"But the word of the Lord endureth forever. And this is the word which by the Gospel is preached unto you." Here is a recognized apostle of Christ claiming that the New Testament, alike with the Old Testament, is the word of God. Christianity's Book is thus all Scripture, old and new. Christianity stands or falls not simply with the four gospels, nor with the records of the doings and sayings of the apostles, but also with Moses and the Prophets and the Psalms. "Search the Scriptures, for they are they which testify of Me." "If ye believe not Moses' writings, how shall ye believe my words?" So says Christ. "The word of

God which yé heard of us, ye received it not as the
word of men, but as it is in truth, the word of
God." So says an apostle of Christ. They go
together. They are equally of God. The Pentateuch and the gospels, the prophecies and the
epistles, the Psalms and the Revelation, Moses
and Matthew, Isaiah and Paul, David and John—
they all point to Christ, preach Christ, are explain-
able only by Christ. Make them Christless and
you make them meaningless. Christianity's Book
is the whole Bible. Christianity's record is all
Scripture. The center of the Bible is the socket
of the cross.

I wish just now to press upon your attention
some features of this book. If you are disposed to
deal honestly with Christianity, and to accept the
challenge to a thoughtful and candid consideration
of its claims, here is where investigation should
begin. An appeal to the record is always in order.
Christianity is to be judged by its recorded principles, by its written law, by its accessible and undeniable truths and facts. Here is the book. It is
only the folly of the fool that will let dust gather
on its unopened lids, and yet denounce or doubt its
claims. To know the claims of any author to
consideration we must look inside his works. To
judge of Christianity with any fairness we must
search these Scriptures.

Many read the Bible every day. Some love to read it. Some read it from a sense of duty. Some, it may be, are actuated by a vague and indefinable and unacknowledged fear that somehow it will go wrong with them if the Bible be not read. Many, in all probability, read it just as the mood takes them ; and many seldom, if ever, read it at all. Whatever may be the truth as to your familiarity, or want of familiarity with this book, I ask you now to look into it a while with me. Not a tithe of its wonders can be even named in a brief hour. No hundred books have been written about as much as this one; and no writer that has written about it claims to have yet fathomed its depths. Surely a book that has made such stir and shown such resource, that has had so much to do with the life of the world, that has been such an acknowledged power in society, that has had so remarkable a history, and that is to-day published in well nigh all the languages of the globe, cannot be without interest to every thoughtful mind as possibly justifying to the fullest extent the imperious and profound claims of Christianity. Our brief glance at only a few of the marvels of this book may compel a change of judgment—may be enough to show that the Bible cannot be accounted for on any other ground than that it is of God!

1. Its *history* commands our attention. It is unique and altogether peculiar. In some of its parts it is by far the oldest book in the world—the earliest production of the human mind now in existence. We have a kind of veneration for antiquity. We cross seas and continents to look with interest and wonder on the work of preceding centuries. But in our homes we have ancient monuments of written language so venerable that there is nothing extant to match them. Take the different parts of the Bible, and consider when they were written, through nearly a score of centuries; by whom they were written—by prince and peasant, by sovereign and slave, scholar and novice, men of letters and men without letters; in what conditions they were written—of affluence and indigence, under widely different states of society, in ages widely apart, treating subjects of limitless sweep and vast significance, going fearlessly down on record both as to the remote past and the remote future, and thus risking exposure both by scientific research and by the progress of events. And yet the authors are all found in harmony, the different parts dove-tail with a wonderful fitness, the same great object pervades them all, the type and the typified, the prophecy and fulfillment, the shadow and the substance, the mysterious contra-

riety of Messianic characteristics, and the mysterious person in whom these opposing and seemingly contradictory characteristics all meet, answer to each other in a marvelous way, and from Genesis to Revelation is unfolded the same great system of truth and duty. How did such a book get into the world? The book is here, itself a miracle. Account for it, will you, without God!

The word "Bible," as many of you know, is from the Greek word βιβλιον, meaning a roll or scroll, *i. e.*, a volume or book, such being the ancient form of a book made from the inner bark of the papyrus, or from parchment. As a plural noun —τα βιβλια—"the books," it was applied in the ancient Greek and Latin churches to the whole collection of sacred or canonical books; but in the English, as in all the modern languages of Europe, it has become a singular noun, το βιβλιον, and thus signifies "The Book." Hence, "the Bible" means, literally, *The Book*, as if there were no other. So that common usage has come undesignedly to make recognition of what it is, and what God designed it to be, *the one book of the world.*

This book began to be some fifteen centuries before Christ. Its first parts were written by Moses, the great Hebrew legislator and law-giver. The

Jews, of all sects, from time immemorial have held
to this view. This tradition is wide-spread, persistent, most ancient and almost unanimous.
Scholars, well-nigh to a man, and after the widest
research, agree in this—that the first five books of
the Bible, called the Pentateuch, must be assigned
to the Mosaic period and must be conceded Mosaic
authorship. Do not let us be alarmed by the jin-
gle of Ingersollisms, and get in a hurry to give up
Moses. In giving up Moses we may be compelled
to give up Christ. If Moses was a fraud, Christ
was, for Christ endorsed him. " If ye believe not
Moses' writings, how shall ye believe my words?"
Subsequent to Moses, additions were made to the
sacred writings from time to time, and all were
held in sacred reverence by the Jewish nation and
most carefully preserved. The Jews were the
guardians of what is called the Old Testament, until
the birth of Christ. For many centuries after, they
had these Scriptures largely under their care.
They copied them with most scrupulous exactness.
" The deep reverence of the Jews for their sacred
books, manifests itself in their numberless rules for
the guidance of copyists in the transcription of the
rolls designed for use in the synagogue service.
They extended to every minute particular; the
quality of the ink and the parchment; the number,

length and breadth of the columns; the number of lines in each column, and the number of words in each line. No word must be written till the copyist had first inspected it in the example before him, and pronounced it aloud; before writing the name of God he must wash his pen; all redundance or defect of letters must be carefully avoided; prose must not be written as verse, or verse as prose; and when the copy has been completed, it must be examined for approval or rejection, within thirty days." When these copyists repeated a word, or wrote down a wrong letter, or blotted the parchment, they never made a correction—they destroyed the skin, and commenced work on another. They could tell the number of times the first letter of the Hebrew alphabet was repeated in the Old Testament. They could give the central letter of each book, for they counted the words and the letters of them all. Though these rules and rigid scrupulosities, superstitious and foolish as some of them seem, bear date subsequent to the beginning of the Christian era, the spirit of reverence for the sacred books which they manifest, assures us that a marvelous and almost miraculous supervision and care were always exercised by the Jews for the preservation and purity of their so-called sacred books. And when we consider that the very writings thus so remarkably preserved, are full of the severest censures upon the nation preserving them, representing the Jewish people as unexampled in their privileges, at the same time without a parallel in their odious idolatries and senseless traditions, God charging them with the wildest ingratitude and spiritual harlotry, and visiting them with the severest chastisement, and holding up their crimes as deserving the just judgment of heaven—when we consider that such a condemning record as this was preserved by the Jews themselves, the evidence of Jewish fidelity in protecting their books from error, seems to be put beyond a question.

The New Testament portion of the Bible, was of course written after Christ's coming, and within the first century. The preservation of this in its essential purity is also established by many excellent proofs, and especially by the discovery of three ancient manuscripts—one, now in the British museum, bearing indubitable evidences of having been written in the fifth century; another, now in the Vatican at Rome, written in the fourth century; and the third, found at a convent on Mt. Sinai, and now at St. Petersburg, also written in the fourth century. These documents have been providentially preserved through all the dangers of fourteen or fifteen centuries, and are now delivered safe in our hands, wonderful witnesses of the general and essential accuracy of our common English bibles. "No simple work of ancient Greek classical literature," says Tischendorf, "can command three such original witnesses as the Sinaitic, Vatican and Alexandrine manuscripts, to the integrity and accuracy of its text." Here then is a book, the oldest in the world, whose construction extended over at least fifteen hundred years, written therefore, in ages widely apart, and by every variety of authorship; its general accuracy certified by almost every possible proof, and handed to us across the waste of thirty centuries. This, of itself, should invest it with surpassing interest.

2. Consider now *the historical character of its contents.* Viewed in the entire sweep of its record, the Bible covers the whole period of time, and embraces the whole destiny of the human race. It does not start with the record of events occurring when its first books were written, but goes back to the world's birth, and tells us how the foundations of the earth were laid. Thence it brings us down the record of time, presenting the general history of the world in the first few chapters, then the special history of the children of Israel, and so it bears us forward through the lapse of ages and

generations, and on by prophecy through the future
to the end of time, revealing at last the judgment,
with its unchangeable issues of life and death, when
the righteous and the wicked shall alike go to their
own place. No other book does this. No other book
has a rational account of the creation of the world,
of the origin of man, of his entire history, and of
his future destiny. Mythology abounds in accounts of creation; but the fabulous and the ridiculous are so intermingled, there is such trifling
about the times and imagined incidents of creation,
such an incongruous mixture presents itself, " that
the very school-boy laughs at these fables as he spells
them out in his Latin or Greek reader." Take
the simple, but sublime imagery of the Bible account of creation, that grand opening declaration,
"In the beginning, God created the heaven and
the earth," and then the formlessness, the darkness
primal, the brooding spirit of God, the omnific
Word giving birth to light, setting fast the firma-
ment, laying the beams of its chambers in the
midst of the waters and hanging the earth upon
nothing; and how is all this transformed and deform-
ed by the traditional cosmogony of the Greek fables,
telling us that from Chaos were born Night and
Erebus, and how from them arose the Ether and
the Day, and how afterward Earth was born,

from whom, and like to itself on all sides surrounding, came starry Ouranos.

The history of the race, also, is to be found nowhere else beyond the lids of the Bible, bearing
here on its very face the impress of accuracy, and
corroborated in all its allusions to geography and
climate, to manners and customs, by subsequent
scientific researches—the very ruins of ancient cities, and the very rubbish of the remote past compelled now to bear witness to the historical correct-
ness of biblical statements.

Very many of its prophecies, too, have been
verified by exact fulfillment, giving us warrant
that the rest of the prophetic record relating
to the world's great moral transformation, the
end of time, the judgment and eternity, will have
like verification. Take the prophecies concerning the Jews, (Leviticus, xxvi; Deuteronomy,
xxviii; Luke, xxi, 24;) and what wonderful fulfillment they have had and *are having!* "Give
me an evidence of Christianity," said a king to one
of his subjects. "The Jews, your majesty," was
the reply. And to-day, over all the world, they
are still fulfilling the word of Scripture. When
Babylon was the glory of kingdoms, Isaiah dared
prophecy of it that it would be swept with the
besom of destruction and never be inhabited. Go

read the words of that prophecy, Isaiah,xiii, 19, 20 and xiv, 23.   Read also the prophecies of Nineveh and of Tyre, and above all, the minute, circumstan-tial,vastly varied and seemingly contradictory proph-ecies of the Messiah, running through and through the Old Testament, and appearing in all its warp and woof.   Then read the facts, the unquestionable and unchallenged facts of history, and see how they match the Word.   Who copied the facts so minutely and so accurately when they were only *history waiting to be made?*. There the facts are, imbedded in writings ages before the events came to pass.   Was this the happy-go-easy guess work of some human imaginations? His-tory that anticipates its facts, and risks all on their fulfillment—who writes it?   Such history is here; Christianity's book, itself a miracle. Account for it, will you, without God!

3.   But, this book challenges attention *as a liter-ary work*; for its grand ideas and glowing imagery, its sublime descriptions, its pathos, its reasoning, stimulating thought and imagination, addressing and gratifying the intellect, the taste, the æsthetic nature.

Persons of fine mental culture are often utterly unaware of the wealth of thought and touching incident there is in the Scripture. But the truth is, as a book for the *mind*, simply, it has no peer in the world. Viewed intellectually, it is incomparably superior to all else men have produced. Just as the earth is crowded with the sublime and the beautiful, so is this book. It has poem and proverb and story and psalm; compact logic and thrilling verse. It is not simply a theological treatise, a code of laws, a religious homily, a dry dictionary and grammar of the language of Canaan; but the Bible—*the Book*—while the only book for the soul, the best book for the mind. I am well aware that many have never looked upon it so. So irksome indeed and so insipid have early association and its begotten prejudices made the book with some, that it has been truly said, " Were they shut up in a parlor with an old directory, and an old almanac, and an old Bible, they would spend the first hour on the almanac, and the next on the directory, and would die of *ennui* before they opened the Bible." This is partly the fault of the friends of the Bible; parents and teachers, and ministers, misusing the Bible; associating it with tasks; compelling its reading at great length and in rigid course, and with no reference to the tastes and aptitudes, and varying needs of children and youths; going with like fidelity and like listlessness through joyless genealogies and joyful psalms, through the merest details of history and touching stories of homes and hearts, making no effort to bring out the beauties and set forth the excellencies and to explain and enforce the precious lessons with which the Bible abounds. But the distaste and disrelish for this book are partly owing to the prejudices of the natural heart against anything distinctively associated with religion.

Christianity's book is full of the choicest gems of thought, combining a variety and richness and rareness to be found in no other volume. What I have said of its construction in different ages, in different countries, by different authors, with widely varying tastes and gifts, and styles of thought and speech, would naturally make it marvelous in its variety and of universal adaptation. And when we come to read the book we find it is so. Do we want logic? We have it, convincing, compact, complete in Paul. Would we be moved by the sublime? There is nothing in the whole compass of human language so full of sublimity as some of the passages in Job and Isaiah and the Psalms and Revelation. Are we fond of aphorism and sententious maxim? Where are these to be found, so full of pith and pungency, so terse, so sharp, so vigorous as in the Proverbs of Solomon? Narrative in its rarest simplicity and beauty, is in the Pentateuch and the gospels. The book of Ruth is a story of filial affection and devotion, which, in touching description, Voltaire himself said there was nothing in Homer or in any other classic writer to equal. If we are charmed with sanguine and hopeful speech, we may catch the spirit of it as we touch the pulse beating in all the words of the ardent and impulsive Peter. If we would calm the vague, dark tumult of our heart's inner sea, and hush the din of earth's angry noises, we may go to the undisturbed stillness of those depths where the thought of the beloved disciple flows "like a molten melody or an abysmal joy." If we would please the fancy we have the tender pastoral. If we would stir the imagination, we have the winged flights of the bold singer of Israel and the triumph songs of God's victors at the Red Sea, and the rapt visions of the seer of Patmos. History, biography, poetry, narrative, incident, argument, sublimity, simplicity, beauty, glory, passion, peace, tenderness, tearfulness, song and story, they are all here. Let me cite you to some of them.

Biography. Is there a better, a purer, a nobler than that of Jesus? Even in the judgment of those who do not believe in the Bible as I believe in it, His is the " greatest soul of all the sons of men," and "there is none born greater than

Jesus," "standing alone," "serene in awful loveliness," "the highest type of man." "Blessed be God," says Theodore Parker, "that so much manliness has been lived out, and stands there yet, a lasting monument to mark how high the tides of divine life have risen in the world." Can any one afford to be ignorant of the history of such a character, so peerless and so alone among men? This one spotless biography, the only one in the world, is found in the Bible.

Vivid description. Is there any classic picture of a thunder-storm to surpass the twenty-ninth Psalm? Listen to it, and see how Jehovah's presence adds grandeur to the majestic ode, and how it must have filled men with a kind of wondering awe as they stood and saw the progress of the storm: " The voice of the Lord is on the sea; the God of glory thundereth; the Lord is on the mighty sea. The voice of the Lord is powerful; the voice of the Lord is full of majesty. The voice of the Lord breaketh the cedars; yea, the Lord breaketh the cedars of Lebanon. The voice of the Lord divideth the flames of fire. The voice of the Lord shaketh the wilderness. The Lord sitteth upon the flood, yea, the Lord sitteth King forever."

The sublime. Where shall we find it if not in the Bible? Go read the petty and crude fancies of ancient fables, trifling about creation, and then turn to the thirty-eighth of Job and listen to the Lord's challenge out of the whirlwind: "Where wast thou when I laid the foundations of the earth? Whereupon are the foundations thereof fastened, and who laid the corner-stone thereof when the stars of the morning sang together, and all the sons of God shouted for joy? Or who shut up the sea with doors in its gushing forth when it issued from the womb? When I made the cloud the garment thereof, and thick darkness a swaddling band for it? When I brake upon it my law, and set bars and doors, and said, 'Hitherto shalt thou come and no farther, and here shall thy proud waves be stayed?' Hast thou commanded the morning? Hast thou caused the dawn to know its place? Where is the way where light dwelleth? Who hath divided a water-course for the over-flowing of waters, or a way for the lightning of thunder? Hath the rain a father? or who hath begotten the drops of dew?"

Figures of speech. Where are they, so beautiful, so eloquent, so graphic, as in the Scriptures? "He looketh on the earth and it trembleth;" that is the earthquake. "He toucheth the hills and they smoke;" that is the volcano. "The pillars of heaven tremble and are astonished at his reproof;" that is the quaking from the thunder of His power. "He hangeth the earth upon nothing;" that is the world swung in its orbit by the word of the Lord.

Tender pastorals, beautiful and touching idyls. There are none made rarer and sweeter than the songs and hymns of the Hebrews. That twenty-third Psalm, "The Lord is my shepherd; I shall not want; He maketh me to lie down in green pastures: yea, though I walk through the valley of the shadow of death, I will fear no evil." O how many timid souls, stepping into the gloom of death's shadowy valley, have grown calm and trustful at the gentle warbling music of this un-surpassed idyl. And what immortal robing has been given to true and tender fidelity in those words of Ruth, "Entreat me not to leave thee, nor to return from following after thee; for whither thou goest I will go, and where thou lodgest I will lodge; thy people shall be my people, and thy God my God; where thou diest I will die, and there will I be buried. The Lord do so to me, and more also, if aught but death part thee and me." The parable of the prodigal son; who can read it and think of finding narrative elsewhere surpassing it in naturalness and simplicity. Paul's account of "love" in his letter to the Corinthians—how it glows and glistens, radiant and beautiful, the one excelling brilliant amidst a remarkable cluster of brilliants! When this gem flashes out in the light it outshines all the rest: " Love suffereth long and is kind. Love envieth not, vaunteth not itself, is not puffed up, seeketh not her own, is not easily provoked, . thinketh no evil, rejoiceth not in iniquity, but rejoiceth in the truth; beareth all things, believeth all things, hopeth all things, endureth all things. Love never faileth." Greece, whose air was redolent of song; Italy, the land of the passions; sages, heroes, poets, honored in every clime—these all have failed to put into their speech the soul of love imprisoned here in Apostolic word and rustling amidst the leaves of the New Testament.

What wonder that the Bible was one of the four volumes which always lay on Byron's table! It is the most thought-suggesting book in the world. No other deals with such grand themes. Painters! Call the roll of the world's masters in this art; where have they gotten their best conceptions? Poets! Name those that men will not let die; from what source have they drawn highest inspiration? Sculptors! Orators! To what one book are these all so much indebted as to the Bible? The most wonderful of histories, the grandest displays of intellectual power, the boldest conceptions of human thought, and scenes transcending in interest and significance and sublimity all other scenes of time are gathered and centered in this book. An English barrister, not himself a religious man, when asked why he put students in law, from the very first, to the study and analysis of the most difficult passages of Scripture, replied, " Because there is nothing else like it in any language for the development of mind and character." Macaulay said, " The English Bible—a book which, if everything else in our language should perish, would alone suffice to show the whole extent of its beauty and power." It is the awakener of thought. When Luther found the Bible, and gave it to the people, schools sprang up all over Germany. The authors of the Cosmos and the Principia here found food for their master minds, and paid homage to the intellectual worth of the Bible. Here Bacon saw how the path of true science led straight up to God. Here Milton bathed his wings, and though upon his sightless orbs, as he lifted them toward heaven the sunbeams played in vain, he of all mortal singers soared nearest the great white throne.

Now tell me, who first thought these thoughts that poets and painters and sculptors and philosophers of all ages have struggled so to set in song and color and marble and system, counting it a glory for which they would be willing to die to give one of these great thoughts complete expression? The thoughts are here in Christianity's book. Account for them, will you, without God!

4. Look now at *the code of morals* or *the standard of morality* found in the Bible.

It is the only true criterion of right and wrong in human conduct. This book's first and great injunction is, " Thou shalt love the Lord thy God with all thy heart." But it is especially of its inculcations with reference to the duties men owe one another that I would now speak. " Thou shalt love thy neighbor as thyself"—this is its fundamental law. " Whatsoever ye would that men should do unto you, do ye even so unto them:" this is its golden rule. By precept and incident and fact and story, it seeks to illustrate and enforce these great central principles. Thus it lays broad and deep the foundations of a virtuous character. Who is thy neighbor? Humanity is thy neighbor, says the Bible. It overrides all distinctions of race or sect, or caste, or color. It hushes feuds. It makes battles impossible; or would, if its principles were carried out. For we cannot love, and bless, and forgive, and return good for evil, and overcome evil with good, and at the same time hate and fight one another. If the Bible had its way, and its standard of morals were recognized and observed in the world, the swords would be beaten into plough-shares and the spears into pruning hooks, the chains would break away from the limbs of all bondmen, and the world's oppressed would go free, justice would take the place of revenge, law of lawlessness, love of hate, and all political and social relations would be ennobled and beautified. This is no mere rhetorical statement. It is the testimony and the truth of history. It is not commerce, not philosophy, not letters; it is the Bible, that human-izes society. In the proudest days of Greece, when reason was lord, and philosophy achieved its no-blest triumphs; and in Corinth, cultivated, polished, scholary, the light of all Greece, but without a bible, Venus was the worshipped goddess, a per-sonification of lust. Egypt was once the seat of the world's best learning—the home of high cul-ture, yet there the first patrons of the arts and sci-ences were brute worshipers. Now if philosophy and letters, and the arts, painting and poetry and sculpture, are the elevating and purifying forces of society, why did they not perform their office in those ancient days of splendor and power? They did their utmost in Greece, but there they only elevated the few, and these they did not purify. Law achieved its utmost in Rome, and though helped by Cicero's system of ethics, the best which pure heathenism ever produced, civil government failed to lift men up into a life of moral purity.

Now let the Bible in. Give it a place among the forces that mould and modify individual and national character. Look where this book has been the freest—where it has been open to the masses, where no priestly tyranny has put a lock upon it. There you see the best forms of government, the largest liberty, the highest social and moral elevation. The people that have had the Bible—from these alone flow the streams that are beautifying the moral wastes in our world. Bible England, Bible Scotland, Bible America, with all their corruption and at so wide a departure as they are from the standard of morals given in the Scriptures, are the great moral levers that are lifting up the nations. Turn your eyes to the Sandwich Islands, to Africa, China, and India, and see what the Bible has done there. It has put tens of thousands of children at school; changed savages into saints; changed barbarism into civilization; vice into virtue, and transformed woman, the degraded, oppressed, enslaved beast of burden, into the angel of the household, loved and honored as a

4

wife and mother, clothed and in her right mind, sitting at the feet of Jesus. Garibaldi being complimented on his agency in securing Italian deliverance, said, " It is the Bible that has freed Italy." France once tried to do without this book—caused it to be tied to the tail of an ass to be dragged in contempt through the street; put a public prostitute on the Bible upon the altar, and worshipped her as the goddess of reason. What was the consequence? Society was reft of its safeguard—the ship of State lost its chart and compass. France was a sea of blood. " France must have a religion," said one of her greatest statesmen. " The republic without a God was quickly stranded," afterwards wrote Lamartine. Liberty, equality and fraternity were the watchwords—but the liberty was license, and the equality was in lawlessness, and the fraternity was a riot of hate and passion. These, too, are the watch-words of the New Testament—the very doctrine of Jesus. But here they are no rhetorical and unmeaning flourish. The liberty is the liberty of sons, and the equality is the equality of brotherhood, and the fraternity is the fraternity of love.

Again I say, the book is here, itself a miracle. It must be accounted for. Deny it to be what it claims to be, a revelation from heaven, and you are landed

in a wilderness of absurdities, and this book, instead
of being a divine and beautiful harmony, is a
bundle of ridiculous and wild contradictions. Take
the way it was made up, so many books, so
many writers, so far apart in history, so widely
differing every way; yet ONE BOOK, with a perfect
unity, by a marvelous interweaving of prophecy
and fulfillment, doctrine and fact, truth and life;
take its historical contents that sweep backward
to creation and forward to judgment, and the truth
of no one of which has yet been successfully
challenged; take its great thoughts that have
been the inspiration of the world's great thinkers,
and the heights and depths of which have never yet
been scaled or fathomed; take its gospel ethics,
bathed in the light and glory and love of Calvary,
and lifting whole peoples up from debasing levels
to high altitudes; take the fact that it is "the
only book that has ever made the circuit of the
globe, holding its own in every important language
or dialect of men," and keeping its voice clear,
ringing and majestic, as it sounds out to the nations
its great truths; take this and vastly more, that
might be said of it, and tell me, who had to do
with it all?   Who wrote this book?

Did bad men write it?   Then we have the best
book in the world, born of fraud.   We have the

devil in the heart of man, coining a speech that has done more to drive the devil out of the heart of man, than all other agencies and forces combined. We have men writing a book that loads with eternal curses the very imposture of which they were guilty in writing it.

Did good men write it? Then we have these good men saying the heavenliest things with a lie in their mouth. We have angels of innocence clothed with damnable hypocrisy; for they say they spake as they were moved of God. They put before their speech, and they stamp upon all their writings, " *Thus saith the Lord.*" How can they say that, and be good men, unless they be wild fanatical enthusiasts, or unless they do speak the truth? Do these men write like fanatics? Does this book read like the hallucinations of dreamers? Ah, these men are neither fools nor knaves. They do tell the truth. Christianity's book is of God. Difficulties! Yes, or there would be no room for faith. Mysteries! Yes, for how could the infinite God communicate with the finite creature, man, without mystery? A God all understood, would be no God at all.

It is only as a divine revelation, thrilling through all its nervous words with the inspiration of Jehovah, that this book discloses the hidings of its power. It is thus that it brings man face to face with eternal realities. It is thus that it tells man what he most needs to know. It is thus that it takes the human soul, marred and dimmed with earthliness, blackened and blasted with the curse of sin, purifies it of its dross, and makes it fit to be worn in the diadem of Jesus. It is thus that it reaches down into the depths of moral defilement and lifts man up to, and makes him like, God. All the literature of the world has no such influence, works no such marvels, kindles no such hopes as this book. It has been well said, and is no burst of rhetorical extravagance, " The sun never sets on its gleaming page. It goes equally to the cottage of the plain man and the palace of the king. It is woven into the literature of the scholar and colors the talk of the street. It enters into men's closets—mingles in all the grief and cheerfulness of life. It blesses us when we are born, and is with us at our bridals and burials. The aching head finds a softer pillow when the Bible lies underneath. It tempers our grief to finer issues. It lifts man above himself. The timid man looking through the glass of Scripture, does not fear to stand alone, to tread the way unknown and distant, to take the death-angel by the hand and bid farewell to wife and babes and home.

Men rest on it their dearest hopes. It tells them of God and of his blessed Son: of earthly duties and of Heavenly rest."

The quaint lines of Izaak Walton have been verified in the experience of milions—

> " Every hour
> I read you, kills a sin,
> Or lets a virtue in
> To fight against it.''

And to-day, more than sixty million copies of the word of God have been issued by the different organizations of the continents.

Well, this does look as if somebody believed in it. It seems to me this answers Strauss' questions in his "Old and New Faith," "Are we still Christians?" and "Have we still a religion?" Wo be to us, if we ever allow a grasping, repressive, wily, ambitious, spirit-enslaving and soul-dwarfing, anathema-hurling, spiritual and temporal despotism to cast this book out or to shut it away from the people by the lock of priestly tyranny. Wo be to us, if in the mad rush for riches and pleasure, our senses are so swept and our minds are so ravished by material gains and problems and philosophies, that we shall lose the spiritual altitudes of justice and joy, and sweet peace to which the word of God has lifted us, and allow ruthless skeptics to tear its dear cross away, and compel us to write " *Vale, vale, in eternum vale,*" over the graves of our dead.

That there is a vast neglect of the Bible, even by those professing to hold it as the rule of their faith and practice, is alas, too true. Its precious ores are not by any means well mined by Christians. They go too often, content with plucking here and there a flower off the surface soil of Scripture, while utterly ignorant of the wealth of fine gold lying underneath.

Some think simply a Sabbath reading will suffice. Some give it a hurried, listless reading once a day. Some yawn over it late at night, when nature is imperiously demanding rest, reading it as a truce to conscience, not caring to sleep and hardly daring to sleep, till they have gone through the form of looking down the page of a Bible, all the while judging in their honest and secret hearts that the Bible is a very dull book. Some, again, it is a joy to know, study the word, give it time and thought, go searching after its hid treasures, make it their daily companion, lift up their prayers in its storied speech, get themselves possessed with its great thoughts of God, get their memories stored with its wondrous truth, get their hearts ravished with its revelations of the Beloved, get their faith fortified with its grand stays and helps: and

such readers as these—blessed be God—such readers as these, walk out on the promises, take cling-
ing and courageous hold of Jesus, are mighty in
the Scriptures and mighty in prayer and mighty
with God! O for a whole Church of such Bible
readers! If we had them, how truth's victories
would multiply as the drops of the morning! If
we had them, what human hearts would be cleft
asunder by the sword of the Spirit!

Neglecter of the Bible, whoever you are, you
are shutting up, and turning your back upon, and
despising the Book of Life. If inclined to be scep-
tical as to this, the best thing you can do is to read
the book in a candid, teachable frame of mind.
You will soon be convinced of its authority, for it
is self-evidencing. A man once sat down to read
it an hour each evening with his wife. In a few
evenings he stopped in the midst of his reading
and said, "Wife, if this book is true, we are
wrong." He read on, and ere long said, "Wife,
if this book is true, we are lost." Riveted to the
book and deeply anxious, he still read, and soon
joyfully exclaimed, "Wife, if this book is true,
we may be saved." It was not many days more
before they were both led through this door of
truth into the kingdom of the truth. This is the
one great end of the book, to tell man of God's

great salvation. My friend, this is no mean thing. There is nothing mean in eternity. There is nothing little in God. There is nothing to be ashamed of in a rational concern about a hereafter. You know, as I know, that your better and higher nature is the deathless nature. If God is a reality, and the soul is a reality, and you are an immortal being, what are you doing with your Bible shut!

If you do not own this book of books, get it, I beg of you. Read it candidly and thoughtfully. Read it with an honest desire to be guided by its teachings. Read it for a mother's or sister's sake. Read it for your souls sake, and truth's, and Christ's. Read it, and you may know how wrong you are. Read it, and you may know how lost you are. Read it, and you may know how you may be saved. Read it, and your name may be read at last, when God's other books shall be opened—read in that Book of Remembrance which God keeps of them that fear the Lord and that think upon his name.

III.

CHRISTIANITY'S CHRIST.

Truly this was the Son of God.—ROMAN CENTURION.

My Lord and my God.—THE APOSTLE THOMAS.

All history is incomprehensible without Him.—RÉNAN.

Here is the urn of destiny, and that urn holds no dead ashes.—H. B. SMITH.

The sea ebbs and flows, but the rock remains unmoved. —MCCHEYNE.

As little as humanity will ever be without religion, as little will it be without Christ.—STRAUSS.

The rose of Sharon and the lily of the valleys;
The chiefest among ten thousand.
                                    —SOLOMON'S SONG.

CHRISTIANITY'S CHRIST.

Effects are not without adequate cause. Nothing was ever begotten of nothing. Institutions that get established and buttressed up in the world are built on something. They have an origin and an originator commensurate with themselves. They are not the product of chance. They do not spring out of chaos, or legend, or myth, and go at a bound to the supremacy of affairs, commanding the allegiance unto death of the best minds of the race. Here is Christianity. Whence came it? What is it? It is a force in the world, a prodigious force. It has revolutionized society. It has lifted man out of himself. It has changed the face of the world. There it lies, imbedded in more than eighteen centuries of human history; and history of no mean sort—the best record of the race. Buddhism and Brahminism are older, and are linked with more peoples. Mohammedanism, not so old, has to do with a greater multitude. The adherents of these systems have outnumbered the adherents of Christianity. Numerically they are at the lead. But if you weigh men, or weigh nations, there are no numbers of either that can be put in the scale against Christendom without kicking the beam. Christianity has held her own, and made her conquests amidst battles of thought, with discussion at white heat. She herself has been a " beam of light shot into chaos," irradiating the darkness and restoring order. She has not thrived amid moral abominations by wearing pitch upon her garments; but her breath has been as a broken alabaster box of ointment. Because of her coming, men have been ennobled and beautified and given new moods of joy. Her truth has held the best mind of humanity —held it and possessed it, and gotten the unreluctant homage of it, against all and most persistent effort of learning and science to make that truth a lie. Christianity has withstood all attacks from all foes and come off victor. There never has been an institution so fiercely and bitterly and relentlessly opposed. A giant and defiant heathenism, a corrupt and bigoted priesthood, a persecuting, world-conquering state, a proud and reasoning philosophy, a subtle and ingenious skepticism, a sneering and malignant infidelity, a plausible and self-recovering humanitarianism, impelled by the hate and the scorn and the pride and the obstinacy of men's natural hearts,—these all in succession, and often conjointly,—have set themselves to the task of rooting Christianity out of the world's life. " The days of this hated religion are numbered " they have shouted, as some fresh foe has entered the arena to make it bite the dust. And yet, to-day, millions rest on it their dearest hopes; it is flinging its forces, with an enthusiasm of energy beyond all precedent, into the very centers of heathenism; it is banding the world with its lines of light; the sun never sets without new record of its conquests; " our best of uttered prayers are in its storied speech;" our grandest thoughts of God are born of its quickening touch; and the best that men know of immortality was brought them in the revelation-hour of this new gospel.

Who gave the world all this? Who founded such an institution? Whence came Christianity? What is its origin? Such a marvel as this is not among men without a sufficient cause. We are in no trouble to trace its history. It has been too mighty a force to be lost sight of. Just about eighteen hundred years it has been in the world, and no more. It has grooved those eighteen hundred years by its unmistakable lines of progress. And, following these, we are taken back by a path that the boldest skeptic does not question, and concerning which there is no historic doubt—to Palestine and Jerusalem.   There we find the origin of Christianity—the founder of this new religion.   He at whose coming all the city was moved, saying "Who is this?" and concerning whom the multitude said in reply, "This is Jesus, the prophet of Nazareth of Galilee"—He is the sufficient cause of this marvel we call Christianity.   Either He, or there is no cause, and history is a lie, and men are mocked with bubbles and fed on husks.   All lines of evidence converge in the Galilean, the record of whose life is in the four gospels.

Christianity before Him was simply prophecy waiting fulfillment, but the prophets all wrote of Him.   Christianity issued out of Him.   There is no Christianity away from Him.   His personality is woven into the very warp and woof of the new religion.   He can no more be wrested from his place in Christianity than Christianity can be wrested from a place in history.   Take Christ out of the gospel, and you take its heart out.   He is the corner stone upon which all Christian work is builded.   Remove Him, and the superstructure topples to ruin.   The prodigious force of Christianity comes from the personality of Him who rode into Jerusalem upon an ass's colt.   This Christ, whoever He is, has not only originated a system, but He has put Himself into it, as its very life, and soul, and power. Other men have established systems, but their personal force has not gone down into them. But so thoroughly, so absolutely, is Christ in the Christian system, that it may be truly said, What Christianity has done Christ has done; what Christianity professes to do, Christ professes to do. If Christianity reveals a way, Christ is the way. If Christianity teaches truth, Christ is the truth. If Christianity brings life, Christ is the life. About the person of Jesus of Nazareth the hottest of the battle between the champions and the opponents of Christianity has raged. This very hour, millions would die for him.

Who is this Christ, therefore, founding Christianity, and permeating it with a personal force that has augmented with the passage of centuries, swaying men's minds and hearts to-day, over all the world, with incomparable and peerless supremacy?

He was a man. He had flesh and bones. He was born in Bethlehem, was raised in Nazareth, and grew to manhood, increasing in wisdom and stature, and in favor with God and man. He ate, and slept, and lived very much as other men. He wearied of toil, and rested. He had special friendships. He sighed and wept. At a comparatively early age he was crucified and buried. Thus far, all agree. The historic Christ has undoubted place in the world. That such a being lived and died is not a subject of controversy. But was He only a man? Let us see.

He was a teacher. "Never man spake like this man." This was the testimony of His enemies. They wondered at the gracious words which proceeded out of His mouth. And this is not report. We do not rely upon legend or tradition for the statement. The words at which men marveled are here in the four gospels. The instruction that seemed so unlike the talk of other men—the teachings of Jesus of Nazareth—are on record; and men read them to-day and marvel still. The civilization of successive and ever advancing centuries has produced no man to speak like this man. Down into the depths of His thought we still go for hidden treasures of wisdom.

Other men, it is true, have been teachers as well as He. There have been prophets, sent of God, with great truths to preach. There have been philosophers, in advance of their age, enunciating principles wonderfully grand and wonderfully pure —profound and imperishable truth; but they have been overtaken and passed. Their thought has been mastered, and thinking has been afterward done in fields they never traversed. But no one has ever yet been in advance of the teachings of the Galilean. Men still study His words and marvel as of old, saying, "Never man spake like this man." "Try Him as we try other teachers,"—says one who nevertheless denies the supernatural in Christ, and charges the Church with making a God of Him—"Try Him as we try other teachers. They deliver their word, find a few waiting for the consolation, who accept the new tidings, follow the new method, and soon go beyond their teacher, though less mighty minds than He. Such is the case with each founder of a school in philosophy, each sect in religion. Though humble men, we see what Socrates and Luther never saw. But eighteen centuries have passed since the sun of humanity rose so high in Jesus. What man, what sect, what Church has mastered His thought, comprehended His method, and so fully applied it to life."

He spake simply. It was not involved and labored speech that so captivated the common people. He spake with precision. His utterances were determinate. It was not with an "if" or a "peradventure" that he brought truth to men. He spake always with the certainty of absolute knowledge, and as out of the depths of His own being. He spake, too, with an apparent ease and opulence of resources, and with a freedom and familiarity that betokened unclouded sight into the mysterious realms of His thought. He spake authoritatively, in the calm consciousness of reserved and measureless power, and as one who felt, however His doctrine was received, and however men heaped their scorn upon it, it would, even as the word of God, abide forever. No wonder Jerusalem was stirred at His coming, and cried out, " Who is this? " No wonder they marveled at His speech, and said, " Whence hath this man this wisdom?" Did they not know Him? Was He not the carpenter's son? Were they not familiar with His life? Had they not seen Him at His trade? And can any good thing come out of Nazareth? " Whence hath this man this wisdom? " Whence, indeed! Nazareth was no Athens. There was no school of prophets there. Philosophy had no seat in that Judean town, wicked to a proverb. How came it about, that this son of toil, with no advantages of learning and no means of culture, flamed at once into the profoundest of the world's teachers, struck fearlessly out into realms of truth, of whose existence the wisest sages had not even guessed, and poured out a doctrine beautiful as the light, sublime as heaven, and true as God. He was a man, but was He only a man?

He was an examplar. Back of His speech was a life. Behind His marvelous doctrine was a marvelous character. His deed was as pure as His word, and both were without spot or blemish. He united in Himself " the sublimest precepts and the divinest practices." In an age of gross wickedness, amid corruption that had changed the house of God to a den of thieves, and transformed worshipers there into "deceitful hucksters of salvation," this pure soul challenged men to prove that He was pitched with the defiling touch of the surrounding iniquity. He charged the Jews with being of their father, the devil, and with doing their father's lusts, and followed it up with the question, " Which of you convinceth Me of sin?" Pollution touched the hem of His garment and blossomed into purity, but the touch left no stain upon His raiment. " I do always those things that please the Father," said He. " The prince of this world cometh, and hath nothing in me," is His own calm assertion of sinlessness. He never repented, for He had nothing to repent of. He wept, but for the sins of others, not for his own. He summed up all His instruction in Himself, and said to the polluted and the lost, " I am the way—follow me." He thus held up Himself as the model of all possible attainment in moral exeellence. And even publicans and harlots grew away from their plague of sin, as they got closer and closer to this sinless Nazarene.

Now other men have lived and died, illustrious for their probity and moral uprightness. But the purest, the saintliest, the most like God, have revealed imperfection, and confessed it. Christ, on the contrary, claimed a perfectly sinless agreement of His will with the will of the Father. "I do always those things which please Him." He says to men everywhere, "Except ye repent, ye shall all likewise perish;" yet He never repents. He places Himself before men as the absolute summit of human perfection, the single example, the light of the world. Again the question returns, Who is this? He is the one spotless soul in the successive millions of the race. He is that, or His gospel is a contradiction and Himself the fittest subject for the scorn he rained upon hypocrisy and pretense. How came innocence and God-likeness to be mirrored there in that surrounding corruption, if Christ was "genuinely human" and no more? He was a man, but was he only a man?

He was a miracle worker. His works astonished men, as well as His words. This young Galilean healed the sick, cleansed lepers, gave sight to the blind, raised the dead. By reason of this, perhaps even more than because of His marvelous doctrine, there went a fame abroad of Him. And so flocked the multitude at one time to see this doer of wonderful works that His enemies, in consternation, said, "What do we? For this Man doeth many miracles. Behold, the world is gone after Him."

He rested His claim to belief upon His works. He challenged investigation of them. He said to men, "Though ye believe not Me, believe the works; and believe Me, for the very works' sake." He distinctly and unequivocally declared that no other man had done among men the works which He had done.

It is true, other men have performed miracles. Prophets and apostles have worked the works of God. But it has always been in distinct recognition of their dependence, with acknowledgment that the miraculous power was delegated and derived. It has been in the name and by the authority of a superior being. But this Galilean miracle-worker did His wonders as if in the opulence of His own resources, and by the might that was in Himself alone. "I say unto thee, arise!" "I will, be thou clean!" "Lazarus, come forth." These are the mandates of inherent and conscious power. There is no dependence here. And no other man

has thus worked the works of God. I know all
this is questioned. I know the very possibility of
proving Christ a miracle-worker is doubted and
denied; but it is at the utter disregard of all con-
sistency. Listen, and see if what I say is not true.

What are the records of the miracles? Are they
" myths or legendary tales that grew up out of the
story-telling and marveling habit of the disciples
of Christ?" Were these miraculous stories gener-
ated within the period of a few years after Christ's
death? Then it was done by mythologic dreamers
of childish credulity, who nevertheless have preserved along with these vagaries and intermingled
with them the record of the only perfect human
character the world has ever known, and a system
of teachings unaffected by a single error, and transcending the dreams of all sages and the talk of all
philosophers.

Surely this is impossible of belief. That such a
character and such teachings as His are found in
the four gospels is convincing evidence of the gen-
uineness of the record of the miracles. Ah, Christ
Himself is the miracle among the miracles—the
miracle of all ages. And so long as He and His
work are imbedded in the world's thought and life,
men will believe in the divine origin of the Christian religion. Christianity in the person of Christ

is its own evidence. His presence is proof of its being from God.

Strauss, who summarily rejects all miracles and prophecies as simply impossible, nevertheless says of Jesus, "He remains the highest model of religion within the reach of our thought, and no perfect piety is possible without His presence in the heart."

Diderot, the French atheistical philosopher, said, in the presence of a company of infidels, "I defy you all, as many as are here, to prepare a tale so simple, and at the same time so sublime and so touching, as the tale of the passion and death of Jesus."

Rousseau, in the same confession where he speaks of the gospel as "full of incredible things," "repugnant to reason," says, "Is it possible that a book at once so simple and so sublime should be the work of man? Is it possible that the sacred personage whose history it contains should be himself a mere man? Where is the man, where the philosopher, who could live and die without weakness and without ostentation? If the life and death of Socrates were those of a sage, the life and death of Jesus were those of a God."

Theodore Parker, who says of Jesus that in certain, as in marvelous works, "Hercules was his equal and Vishnu his superior," nevertheless adds, "Consider what a work His words and deeds have wrought in the world. Remember that the greatest minds have seen no farther, and added nothing to the doctrines of religion; that the richest hearts have felt no deeper, and added nothing to the sentiment of religion; have set no loftier aim, no truer method than His of perfect love to God and man. Measure Him by the shadow He has cast into the world—no, by the light He has shed upon it. Shall we be told that such a man never lived—that the whole story is a lie? Suppose that Plato and Newton had never lived. But who did their wonders and thought their thoughts? It takes a Newton to forge a Newton. What man could have fabricated Jesus? None but a Jesus."

And Renan, repudiating the supernatural in the recorded life of Jesus, and compelled in the repudiation to speak of Christ as acting on "false views," with much "self-deception," a miracle-worker and exorcist in spite of himself, and only for the purpose of innocent fraud, nevertheless says of Jesus, "He founded the pure worship, of no age or no clime, which shall be that of all lofty souls to the end of time." "Repose now in Thy glory, noble founder! Thy work is finished. Thy divinity is established. Fear no more to see the edifice

of Thy labors fall by any fault. Henceforth, beyond the range of frailty, Thou shalt witness from
the heights of divine peace the infinite results of
Thine acts. For thousands of years the world will
defend Thee. Banner of our contests, Thou shalt
be the standard about which the hottest battle will
be given. A thousand times more alive, a thous-
and times more beloved since Thy death than during Thy passage here below, Thou shalt become
the corner-stone of humanity so entirely that to
tear Thy name from this world would be to rend
it from its foundations. Complete conqueror of
death, take possession of Thy kingdom, whither
shall follow Thee by the royal road which Thou
has traced, ages of worshipers."

Can eulogy go farther than this? Mind you, it
is wrung from the enemies of Christianity. They
are forced to say what shall be done with Christianity's Christ; for here He is in the four gospels.
They must eulogize Him. He compels the homage by His peerless record. So they say, "His divinity is established"; they make Him "the corner-stone of humanity," and give Him "ages of
worshipers;" they say "the greatest minds have
seen no farther," that whatever the coming surprise, "He will never be surpassed;" they make no
"perfect piety" possible "without His presence in

the heart," and declare His life and death to be
those of a God: they do all this, and lift Him utterly out of the order of nature, and yet make it
impossible for Him to *do* anything out of the order
of nature. They admit this greatest of all miracles—such a character, in such an age, pouring out
such a doctrine; and yet deny the miracles He
wrought! How came such a perfect character, so
perfectly portrayed, in such an age and country,
and by such writers—how came it there in the
New Testament? If it was not real, then those
four plain men devised and arranged together and
gave to the world what it has been impossible for
any genius of any age to portray. They did that,
and simply nothing else. They concocted a life
of Christ, the four of them together, dove-tailed
their narrative so as to make the most consummate
portraiture in all literature—did that and died.
Surely the miracle of all ages is this—that such a
Being is in the gospel record; one who ever since
that record was written has been directing the
world's life, shaping the world's history, commanding the world's thought, subduing the world's
kingdoms, overthrowing the world's idolatries. He
was a man. But was He only a man?

He was a martyr. He witnessed to the truth, and
sealed the testimony with His blood. He was not a

prophet of smooth things. Holy and full of love as He was, the antagonism of His nature to evil was deep and uncompromising. He had indignation at the world's wrong. He flashed out His rebukes of hypocrisy and Pharisaic pride with a burning earnestness and an unmasking fidelity that won him no favor among the wearers of broad phylacteries and the children of the devil. They hated Him and hated His doctrine. They sought to lay their hands upon Him and put Him to death. At last they found their opportunity and seized it. And after only three years of public ministry, Christ suffered martyrdom. His enemies seized Him, went through with a mockery of trial, secured sentence of condemnation, and killed Him. He died with a prayer upon His lips for His murderers.

If this were all, His martyrdom would not be singular. For other men have died because of their fidelity to the truth. Prophets of God are often doomed to seal their testimony with blood. By the stake and the cross, by the rack and the fagot, many heroic souls have witnessed to the truth, and stood for its vindication even unto death. And they have done it, too, in such sustained triumph and such joy of their martyrdom that their crosses have seemed to them but steps into heaven, the ascending flames but chariots of fire by which they were borne up to God. So that in the mere matter of physical suffering in the hour of death, there have been martyrs who have seemed to endure their martyrdom with even greater heroism than Christ. If this were all, therefore, His death would not be singular. But it is not all.

He predicts his own death. He talks calmly of it. Yes, He makes it the basis of all His triumphs. He puts beforehand, as the sign and pledge of victory, what all other men would regard as the token of utter defeat. He declares that the grand idea of His mission is the establishment of a kingdom—a kingdom over men's minds, a universal kingdom, and that this kingdom is to spread—but not in a day, not in a lifetime. He, Himself, is to die; but His death is to be the grand attractive power by which men are to be influenced to yield to His supremacy. "And I, if I be lifted up, will draw all men unto me," is the astonishing declaration of this carpenter of Galilee. And this He said, signifying what death he should die. "Except a corn of wheat fall into the ground and die it abideth alone," is His way of telling those about Him of his marvelous expectation, viz., that death, with Him, is to be the sowing before a great harvest, the seed of His great empire. What martyr, in prospect of martyrdom, ever ventured upon such ground as this? But this uneducated village mechanic goes farther still. He gathers a few friends in an upper room at Jerusalem and celebrates there the Jewish Passover. He takes the Paschal cup and says to those present, "Divide it among yourselves; break it up; do with it as you please; I abrogate the feast. I set aside this solemn institution, revered though it has been, as ordained of God, and established for centuries. I call you now to the celebration of another feast." And He takes bread and blesses and breaks it, saying, "This is My body which is given for you." He takes wine and pours it out, saying, "This is my blood which is shed for you. This do in remembrance of Me." He here puts away forever a religious custom, "interwoven with all the policies of the state and all the feelings of the fireside," and substitutes—what? A feast to perpetuate the memory of His own death, the elements of which symbolize His broken body and shed blood. What His enemies are seeking for and are bent on with malice of hell in their hearts, He calmly in that upper room takes steps to have remembered forever. What the world counts ignominious and shameful He means shall be counted by His friends a glory and honor. He thus undertakes utterly to reverse the judgment of mankind concerning His crucifixion, and to make of His martyrdom the most significant and most meaning fact in his marvelous career, and the one of all others to be most fondly and most holily remembered.

Is there not something here transcending any human example? Other men have said, " If I could only live I would establish and perpetuate an empire." This Christ of Galilee says, " My death shall do it." Other martyrs have died in simple fidelity to truth. This martyr dies that He may make His truth mighty over all hearts. He was a man, but was He only a man?

Think again. This Galilean came forth amidst the moral darkness of a corrupt age. He grew to manhood in a town of ill-repute. He left His work-shop at the age of thirty, and forthwith He became author and founder of a religion so pure, it might have had birth in heaven of God. He placed himself at the head of Christianity, permeated it with His personal force, and for eighteen centuries that force has been augmenting until millions now yield Him the unreluctant homage of their fondest affections. This artisan, moreover, fresh from His toil, in three years, gave the world the sublimest doctrines of the soul, of immortality, of God and His fatherhood, of pardon and reconciliation. He discoursed of these with an ease and freedom, with a spiritual opulence and power, with a beauty and fullness and precision and authority, that more than realized the dream of sages and prophets. Along with these imperishable ideas, he brought before men an unsullied, spotless life—a soul unsoiled by evil. He stands as the ideal of humanity—the one perfect example of all time. He did many mighty and miraculous works, and He did them by His own inherent and unborrowed power. There the record of the miracles is in the record of His life. The miraculous can not be torn away without tearing Christ away. The marvel and miracle are as much in the words as in the works. He did those wonders, who thought those thoughts. And when He died His martyr's death, He felt and He said that His dying should be the sign and pledge of His world-wide triumph.

"Who is this?" asked the multitude at Jerusalem. "Who is this?" I ask to-day. He is the carpenter's son, but He is no more? Could He have lifted Himself so out of the succession of men, out of the line of nature, if He had been only human? Could He have stood at the head of the world for eighteen hundred years, and yet be nothing more than the son of Joseph and Mary?

It has been recently affirmed in one of our public prints that Krishnu, a god of the Hindoos, the

6

incarnation of Vishnu, is a " savior almost exactly
like ours and six hundred years older." What shall
be thought of this affirmation in the face of these
two facts: First, that modern scholarship places
the origin of these fictions of Krishnu, that bear
any resemblance at all to Christ, far within the
Christian era. Second, that this Hindoo god Krishnu is a moral monster; that, while many of the
teachings attributed to him have a high morality,
he is represented as sporting in lascivious and lust-
ful license; that the worst scenes of his life are not
fit to be told; that entire dependence on him by
his worshipers not only obviates the necessity of
virtue but sanctifies vice; and that he is responsi-
ble for some of the most licentious of all the Hindoo feasts.

And yet we are asked " to explain why our
Christ is the only true savior, when the Hindoos
have one almost exactly like ours and six hundred
years older!" Are these the shifts to which infidelity is driven? And is this the way in which an
honest skepticism would meet the intelligence and
decency of our time? If Christ was like Krishnu,
then truth lies, honesty cheats, sincerity deceives,
purity defiles. As well might it be said black is
white, and up is down, and right is wrong, and
something is nothing. No. Christ is alone. The

most destructive criticism has not been able to de-throne Him as the incarnation of perfect holiness. The most scholarly research has been unable to find any human conception to compare with Him. The waves of a tossing and restless sea of unbelief break at His feet, and He stands still the supreme model, the inspiration of great souls, the rest of the weary, the fragrance of all Christendom, the one divine flower in the garden of God!

Strange things meet in him! With the most boundless self-assertion, He is the very model of humility. He offers forgiveness; He never seeks it. He exhibits superhuman power, yet with all the sweet and attractive beauty of gentleness. He says that which only God could know was true. He does that which only God has a right to do. If He did not dwell in the bosom of God, if He was not on equality with God, then his forgiveness of sins and his talk about power over his own life to lay it down and to take it again, and his general assumption of divine prerogatives, was blasphemy. Browning has well said:

> "If Christ, as thou affirmest, be of man,
> Mere man—the first and best, but nothing more;
> Account Him for reward of what he was,
> Now and forever wretchedest of all.
> Call Christ, then, the illimitable God,
> Or Lost!"

There is no middle ground. Christ was either the grandest, guiltiest of impostors, by a marvelous and most subtle refinement of wickedness, or he was God "manifest in the flesh." Only by this latter belief do we enter into the higher harmonies of His person, where every seeming contradiction vanishes away, and the blaze of miracles in which He was born and lived and died, seems but the natural and fitting manifestation attending His coming, and stay and departure.

"He is beside himself," said the men of the garnished sepulchre sort. "He hath a devil!" shouted the phylacteried Pharisees. "He is mad! He is in league with Beelzebub! He is guilty of death!" charged the shriveled conservators of the old religion. "Thou art the son of the living God!" reverently said an unlettered fisherman, who had been summoned by this divine Teacher to a life divine and beautiful. Which was right, the Pharisees or the fisherman? Let Christianity answer with her centuries of peerless history. Let the Christian world answer which to-day, worshiping Him equally with the Father, names Him Son of God! Let the millions of hearts answer that think of Him in each returning Christmas time as the divinest gift with which humanity has ever been blessed. Peter's reverent confession is the accepted creed of Christendom. But you may look, and you will not find, the world over, a descendant of the Pharisees who believes Christ was beside himself and leagued with the devil.

Leagued with the devil, indeed, when he came to destroy the works of the devil! Is Satan divided against himself? Shall a devil cast out devils? No! This teacher and exemplar and miracle-worker and martyr, came and taught, and lived and died, to meet a deep necessity. He saw the woe into which man had plunged. He saw the ruin sin had made. The woe was too deep for human specific. The ruin was that of an immortal soul. The ruin was wrought in the power of an endless death. So this Christ came, as He needed to come to repair the ruin, with "the power of an endless life." The ruin was a thinking ruin, the ruin of a soul-temple; and so he came to restore it who first made the immortal temple. And the builder and maker was God! O, how many temples have been builded anew by this divine Architect? Out of how many hearts He has sent evil possessions, that legions of angels might come in.

Sinner, if thou knewest the gift of God, and who it is that saith to thee, "Behold, I stand at the door and knock," thou wouldst have opened the gates of thy ruined temple long ago, to let in this heavenly builder. Listen now. He knocks again. Here, in the hush of this still hour, He waits to be received and welcomed. Peace like a river, joy such as angels do not know, hope full of an ever-brightening and evermore blessed immortali-ty—all heavenly benediction would be thine—" if thou knewest the gift of God!"

IV.

CHRISTIANITY A GOSPEL OF DEFINITENESS.

I know whom I have belived.—PAUL.

Christianity is more than history. It is also a system of truths. Every event which its history records, either is a truth, or suggests a truth, or expresses a truth, which man needs to assent to or to put into practice.—NOAH PORTER.

God so loved the world that He gave His only begotten Son. That whosoever believeth in Him should not perish, but have everlasting life. For God sent not His Son into the world to condemn the world, but that the world through Him might be saved.—JESUS CHRIST.

The two beings the most nearly related to each other in the whole universe—God and man—who were so awfully es· tranged, are brought together reconciled.—YOUNG.

i

CHRISTIANITY A GOSPEL OF DEFINITE-NESS.

What is Christianity? Who are Christians? Is there an answer possible to these questions that shall be at the same time definite and scriptural? One would think there ought to be. Men do not commonly build on shadows. Vagueness is a poor solid for feet of faith. To commit one's self to a gospel of indefiniteness is like taking a leap into the dark. Besides, vague truths get no deathless hold of consciences or hearts. It is only for definite convictions men are willing to die. They will not risk much on a "perhaps." They cannot rest much in a preadventure. The Christ upon whom they hang their dearest hopes must not be in a haze. " I know whom I have belived," is the creed of all stalwart souls. The faith that conquers is the faith that grasps something, and that can tell what it is.

Here is Christianity. It has done some revolutionary things in the world. It makes some imperious claims. We have listened to its challenge.

We have looked at its book of instructions. We have considered who Christ is, its founder. Does this Christ come " filled with the spirit and words of indefiniteness?" Is this book so " wrapped in the clouds of a great mystery," and has it a voice so uncertain, " uttering only vague terms," that we are barred forever from " the hope of knowing in this world what Christ was, what heaven and hell are, and who will go at last to either place?"

So it has been lately said; and we are bidden, with soothing balm and some touches of Oriental rhetoric, to " sleep sweetly in the midst of a grave mystery," for "only in a vague Christianity can we find peace." My friends, if this be true, we have a revelation that reveals nothing, we have an army without a battle-cry, a church without fixed beliefs, doctrines dissolving in mist, shadow for substance, a jelly-fish theology, a gospel of mush.

But is it true? Is this the ring of that glorious gospel of the blessed God, of which the goodly company of the apostles spoke and wrote with such passionate fervor? It may do for a lullaby. But life is a battle, not a hymn. And when the struggle is ended, and men walk out toward eternity, they want to know where they are placing their feet!

What is Christianity? Who are Christians? It

is time the sharp outlines of the old faith were cut
again in the public mind and stamped again upon
the public conscience. Thomas Buckle and Herbert
Spencer are seriously classed among the most
brilliant writers in the Christian ranks of our age.
Men who look upon the Bible as they look upon
Plato's " Phaedo," or the Koran of Mohammed, or
the writings of Confucius, do not hesitate to call
themselves Christians. They do not worship the
Bible, nor yet Christ. They do not go to church.
What of that? The great thing is to be a Christian. We have a so-called " absolute Christianity,"
a " broad-church Christianity," a " liberal Christianity," and just now a " coming Christianity," of
which "indefiniteness is to be the quality." But
can a man believe nothing and be a Christian? Is
Christianity summed up in gentlemanliness and
good breeding, and neighborly kindness, and an
upright life? Or may a man be graceful and yet
graceless? If it be said that Christianity is a life,
must not a life have some law? Life for what?
For whom? To what ends? On what basis?
Rightly to define Christian life is clearly to define
Christianity.

Now if Christianity has any vital fundamental
ideas, any central and essential truths, where
should we look for them? Manifestly, in Chris-

tianity's book, the Bible, and to Christianity's founder, Christ. Away, then, with theories, and fancies, and guesses and wishes. Let us go to the record. Here is the Book. Here speaks the Christ. Let us see what they have to say, and weigh our words as those who are buying the truth.

In the Book, by the Christ, John 3:14–17, we find these words: "As Moses lifted up the serpent in the wilderness, even so must the Son of Man be lifted up, that whosoever believeth in Him should not perish but have eternal life. For God so loved the world that He gave his only begotten Son that whosoever believeth in Him should not perish but have everlasting life. For God sent not his Son into the world to condemn the world, but that the world through Him might be saved."

Luther called these words of Christ "the Bible in miniature." They have been deemed by the devout and scholarly of the Christian ages an epitome of the gospel. If there be any soul to Christianity, it is here.

They give us, first of all, the source of Christianity. It was born of God's great heart of love. "God so loved the world." Remember that, my friends, when men rail at these scriptures, and call the gospel a damnation, and God a tyrant. The words next give us the person sent—" the Son of Man," " the Son of God."   Next, the purpose of the sending—salvation, " that the world through Him might be saved."   Next, the character of the salvation—not from misfortune, from ignorance, from trouble, but from death, that men " should not perish;" and as " not to perish" has for its expressed and exact equivalent "everlasting life," the exact equivalent of "to perish" must be everlasting death.   Next, the words give us the necessary ground and way of salvation, Christ's sacrifice unto death on the cross—"even so must the Son of Man be lifted up."   Next and last, the words give us the subjects of salvation —"whosoever believeth in Him," i. e., in this Son of Man lifted up on the cross.   Here then we have the person of the Savior, and the purpose, the character, the ground, and the subjects of His salvation; or *Jesus Christ, Son of Man and Son of God, a power unto salvation from endless death, by atoning sacrifice through faith.*

This, I make bold to say, is the essential substance of Christianity.   Wrapped up in this pregnant statement are all its central and fundamental truths.   There are other truths, but they are subordinate.   These are chief and vital.   These must be preached if Christ is preached.   I know we are charged with foisting dry and dead doctrines on the church in place of the graces and charities and duties of a practical piety. I know we are charged with twisting Christianity from its Christ-fashioned original of practical and beautifying life into soulless and un-Christ-like creeds. Well, here is our creed. There is some definiteness about it, surely. Let us see if it is un-Christ-like. Let us see if the gospel is not ribbed all about and interpenetrated through and through with these grand redemptive thoughts. Let us see if this is not the golden thread upon which all God's precious promises are strung.

Jesus Christ, Son of Man and Son of God, a power unto salvation from endless death by atoning sacrifice through faith. We will take this sentence to pieces, and undertake to explain and justify each part by an appeal to the four gospels.

1. The person, Jesus Christ. At the very basis of any true notion of Christianity must be a true notion of Christ. Christianity without Christ would be a body without a soul, light without a sun, history without civilization, a universe without a God. Go and " untwist all the beams of light in the sky," and get at and expunge one of the colors fixed there of God! Let an army be set to changing the smallest truth of mathematics! Either

would be as easy as getting the person of Christ
out of the gospel.   But what kind of a person is
He?   How was He constituted who is called
Christ?   A true conception of Him makes the
whole realm of Christian truth luminous.   Wrong
view here is the secret and source of wrong view
as to well-nigh all else in the Christian system.

First, as " Son of Man," He was perfect in His
humanity, absolutely without flaw, a real man of
body, soul, and spirit; tempted, tried, and touched
with the feeling of human infirmities, yet without
sin.   If He were a sinner, the whole Christian
scheme fall.   If He ever sinned He needed a
Savior, and could not therefore even save Himself.
He claimed sinlessness.   " I do always those things
which please the Father."   " The prince of this
world cometh and hath nothing in Me."   He
challenged His enemies to convince Him of sin.
He never uttered a word of self-reproach.   Not
one sign did He ever give, not one word ever fell
from His lips, either to man or to God, which expressed or implied the sense of a single defect.
And yet, though He pronounced all other men sinners, and said He Himself was absolutely without
sin, He maintained the merit of most peculiar
modesty, and of all men has been regarded as "the
meek and lowly of heart."   No one ever charged

Him with conceit. Put these things together—this matchless claim and this unchallenged, everywhere conceded, and matchless modesty—and tell me, was Christ a sinner? If a sinner, He knew He was. But such hypocrisy, for such purpose, to unfold a character of beauty and harmony without the approach of rivalry among the sons of men, is simply impossible of belief. No. Christ was the advent of a perfect man. Behold the Lamb without blemish and without spot, the Holy One, the Just, who did no sin, neither was guile found in His mouth, harmless, undefiled, separate from sinners. But all the truth concerning Christ is not told when this is told.

As " Son of God, " Christ was perfect in His divinity—divine-human, God manifest in the flesh. It is not my purpose, now, to go into a critical exegesis and analysis of single texts to prove that this is the teaching of the gospels. Let learning fortify the evidence by such minute and careful dissection. But the gospel biography of Jesus, taken as a whole, is what I would ask you to look at. And instead of setting forth the beautiful and harmonious and peerless life which even Christ's enemies concede is there, that biography is a jumble of absurdities, and full of utterly irreconcilable statements, if Jesus be not God. Group together the personal assertions and claims of Jesus, and see. " He distinctly, repeatedly, energetically preaches Himself." He says; " I am the bread of life. " "I am the living bread that came down from heaven." " I am the light of the world." " I am the way, the truth, the life." Not " I am come to show the the way." "I Myself am the way." Not to teach truth. "I Myself am the truth. " Not to give life. " I Myself am the life." He says, " If ye ask any thing in My name I will do it. " He claims to be the lord of the realm of death. He will Himself awake the sleeping dead. All that are in their graves shall hear his voice. He encourages men to trust in Him as they trust in God; to believe in Him as they believe in God; to honor Him as they honor God. He commands, He does not simply invite, discipleship. Men receive His message by giving themselves up to Him. They reject it by rejecting Him. No rival claim, no natural affection, may interpose between Himself and the soul of one who would be His disciple. He lays His hand upon all the dearest and most tender relationships of life, upon all the fondest and most treasured loves of the human soul, and demands a precedent and superior love, saying, " He that loveth father or mother more than Me is not worthy of Me." All radiates from Himself. All converges

7

toward Himself. He is the supreme Lord of Life. He distinctly claims such lordship. He asserts equality with the Father, and for this the Jews take up stones to stone Him for blasphemy, " Because, " said they, " that Thou being a man makest Thyself God." Jesus does not deny that He claimed equality with God, but He does deny that this was blasphemy. It would have been that, or the raving of a demented enthusiast, if He were not divine. He claims divine prerogatives, asserting the same power for Himself that He asserts for the Father. He accepts without rebuke the glowing confession of Thomas, " My Lord and my God. "

Now put any mere creature — any purely human teacher, the noblest and the best—to saying these things. Let him come to the front, ye deniers of the divine incarnation; place him before the world. It is held that other men have said as divine things as Jesus. It is held that the world is outgrowing His talk; that His religion, like all others, must give way to human development; that Christianity is but one step onward in humanity's progress, and by no means the last. Produce the sage, then, the philosopher, the schoolman, the scientist, who will say to men, " Follow me. Believe in me. I am the light of the world. Ye are from beneath. I am from above. Behold a greater than Solomon is here. I have power to lay down my life and to take it again. I am that living bread of which if any man eat he shall live forever. It is not possible to love God and not love me. And no man can come to God but by me." Do we not know that no human being on earth could set up the least of these astounding pretensions without winning the pity or the contempt of mankind? Yet from Jesus Christ they come over and over again. And they do not surprise us nor give rise to the least feeling of incongruity. Nay, human hearts read the gospel record and connect with Him who made these transcendent and awful claims the rarest and sweetest humility that ever blossomed in character among all the sons of men. This is simply and absolutely impossible on any other ground than that Christ is the divine man and the incarnate God in one undivided person. This, therefore, is the person sent of the Father—God manifest in the flesh.

2. But such a person must be thus constituted for some great reason. God is manifest in the flesh for a purpose. What is this purpose? Christ tells us. "God sent His Son into the world that the world through Him might be saved." He says

elsewhere, " The Son of Man is come to save. " He says again of His people, "I give unto them eternal life." " Those that come to Me shall never perish. " " Whosoever believeth in Me shall have everlasting life." A name is given Him out of heaven, that distinctly declares His mission. He is called " Jesus, " Savior. Christ is therefore a power unto salvation._ Christ did not come simply or mainly with a system of education. Christianity is no scheme of moral reform, such as other teachers have brought to the world. Jesus did not come to teach truth, as if that were all men needed. That would imply the possibility of *educating* the soul out of its difficulty and doom. He came for rescue. If Christianity were only a development, then Christ was not needed. If Christianity were only a scheme of morals, then the divine incarnation was a thing superfluous. Some great need must be found to match that great provision. Any crea- ture of God, from any world of His, could have been sent to tell us the truth, or to effect reform, if that were all that was had in view in Christ's coming. It was not all. Christ came to save.

But to save from what? From *perishing*, Jesus says. He was sent of God that men " should not perish. " Twice, in these few words, He gives this thought a solemn emphasis. And over against perishing He places salvation, and in each case He calls the salvation "everlasting life." What must the perishing be but everlasting death? This is what the salvation is from. Not from misfortune, so much, nor from trouble, nor from ignorance, nor from degradation; all these, but infinitely more, from endless death and sin. From the death, the sting of which is sin, and from the sin, the wages of which is death.

Never mind, now, microscopic investigation in philology to determine the exact shade of meaning of two or three Greek words. That has its place and worth. But take the trend of these gospels. Listen to the sad music of these tender, solemn, inexpressibly sad words. They fell from the lips of Christ alone. I quote no other. And not a scholar with any claim to competency challenges one of them as an interpolation. "Except a man be born again he cannot see the kingdom of God." "I never knew you; depart from Me, ye workers of iniquity." "Depart from Me, ye cursed, into everlasting fire." "As, therefore, the tares are gathered and burned in the fire, so shall it be in the end of this world." "And these shall go away into everlasting punishment." "For I say unto you that none of these which were bidden shall taste of My supper." "The door was shut." Do you not see the terrible irreversibleness and dread finality of all this? Surely Christ is a power unto salvation from endless death.

3. But what is the ground or way of salvation? Where does the gospel record put the power of Christ to save? Again it is Himself who tells us, "As Moses lifted up the serpent in the wilderness, even so must the Son of Man be lifted up." Afterward He said: " My flesh will I give for the life of the world." "I am the good shepherd. * * * The good shepherd giveth his life for the sheep." " The Son of Man came not to be ministered unto, but to minister, and to give his life a ransom for many." And when the eventful hour approached, He said, "Now is my soul troubled. Now is the crisis of this world. Except a corn of wheat fall into the ground and die, it abideth alone; but if it die, it bringeth forth much fruit. . . . And I, if I be lifted up from the earth,"—if I die—die on the cross—" will draw all men unto me."

Here, then, from the lips of Christ Himself, is the doctrine that He came to save men by dying for them; that the hour of His death on the cross was the crisis hour of this world—the pivotal point in the history of the human race. He nowhere intimates that His power to save lies in the wisdom of His instruction. He nowhere intimates that His power to save lies in His blameless example. He lived a holy life indeed—the one model of all time. He gave divine instruction, indeed—out of His mouth flowed gracious and wondrous speech. But this is not Christianity's inner and essential substance. It drops out the vital truth of the atoning efficacy and attractive power of Christ's cross. There Jesus put His saving power. "The Son of Man must be lifted up, that"—to the end that, in order that—" whosoever believeth in Him should not perish." He who preaches Christianity, therefore, must preach an atoning sacrifice—Christ, not only, but Christ crucified. Fulsome laudation of the character and life of Jesus will not answer. Yielding Him admiration and tears will not do. The recognition of Him as a divine incarnation, leaves still a mutilated gospel. The men that come to Him saying, "Rabbi, we know that thou art a teacher come from God; for no man can do these miracles that thou doest except God be with him," are not the men that have yielded yet the homage and the belief that are vital. Christ crucified—He alone is the power of God unto salvation. Christianity's central fact is Calvary's cross. Hence the apostolic emphasis put upon this idea. Those first preachers of Jesus, how they gloried in the cross! How they set forth Jesus crucified, and lifted to the sight of men the Lamb of God, as a sacrifice and a propitiation for sin! How they dwelt upon the death of their Lord as the necessity of the world, and as alike the foundation and the hope of salvation! How they boldly cast their all for time and eternity upon the redeeming and cleansing power of Christ's blood! Place their preaching along-side this modern preaching of a gospel of indefiniteness, and see if it is not " another gospel." Put the two side by side—the one as found in the pages of the New Testament, and the other as found in the pages of the morning paper. Read through the lines, or between the lines, or behind the lines, and see what a great gulf is between the gospel of indefiniteness and the gospel of the scriptures; not simply as to style—that we might expect; not simply as to methods of illustration—that we might expect; but as to *the blood of the atonement!* Tell me, he who blots out that blood, or ignores it, in his ministry, in his belief, in his life, what is there left to blot his sins out? Does he preach, does he believe, does he live Christianity? He who tears down the cross, what is there left to lift him to heaven? He who drops this vital, essential fact out of Christianity, and makes the cross of Christ of none effect, is recreant to Christianity. He perverts and falsifies the truth as it is in Jesus. He may call himself a Christian, but in the specific, gospel sense he is anything else. He is sailing under false colors. He may wear the name, but of him the Lord, whose vicarious sacrifice he rejects, will say at last, "I never knew you." The church claiming to be a Christian church, is false to the title, if she make the cross of Christ of none effect.

Whatever else men may teach, therefore, and whatever else they may believe, if they do not teach and if they do not believe Christ as a power of God unto salvation by atoning sacrifice, they do not teach and believe Christianity. This, according to the express words of Christ, as we have shown, this is Christianity—its central, essential, fundamental truth. This, of all else, was preached boldly, constantly, eloquently, and with prodigious power by the immediate disciples of Christ, as their writings and as historical records show. They determined not to know anything among men save Jesus Christ and Him crucified. God forbid, said the chief apostle, that I should glory save in the cross of our Lord Jesus Christ. This was the secret of their success, and it has been the potent truth of Christ's gospel ever since; the Lamb of God slain for the propitiation of sin; the blood of Jesus shed for the cleansing of all guilty and sin-stained hearts; Christ crucified the power of God unto salvation. Wherever this has been expunged from the creed and the life, there has been no aggressive force, no regenerative and transforming power, no winning of men from the ways of sin to a life with God.

Hear, now, the confession of so-called liberal Christianity, made with refreshing frankness and boldness by one of its chief organs. "Liberal Christianity," it says, "makes no headway among coarse, uneducated, and unthinking people. Its necessary condition of success is a public possessing something beyond the average amount of culture, intellectually and morally." Upon its own confession, therefore, for the vast majority of mankind, this liberal Christianity is utterly unfit. Can it be, then, that this is the gospel Christ commanded his disciples to go into all the world and preach to every creature? Is this the Christianity that the common people heard gladly in Christ's time, that even reached publicans and harlots, and lifted them to a life of purity and piety, divine and beautiful? Is it Christianity at all? Is it not rather a libel on this free and glorious gospel of Jesus, adapted to man as he is everywhere, reaching down to the lowest and vilest, and capable of lifting them up to divine heights of grace and glory? Call it what you will, but do not call this thing of boasted culture, designed only for the elevated and intellectual few—

do not call this Christianity. That is giving it the stolen livery of the very Christ whose work it persistently ignores and denies. Nor call anything else Christianity that does not hold fast to this cardinal truth: Christ, the divine-human, God manifest in the flesh, a power unto salvation by atoning, expiatory sacrifice.

4. But who are the subjects of this salvation? "Every one that believeth." Jesus is a power unto salvation through faith alone. It is Jesus Christ Himself who repeats again and again with most explicit and unmistakable definiteness this gospel truth. Twice, in the brief compass of the sentence we are taking to pieces, it is distinctly affirmed that God gave His Son that "whosoever believeth in Him should not perish." A little farther on Jesus says, "He that believeth not is condemned already, because he hath not believed." He said again, "he that believeth on me shall never thirst." And again, " This is the will of Him that sent me, that every one who seeth the Son and believeth on him may have everlasting life." And again, "He that believeth in me, though he were dead, yet shall he live; and he that liveth and believeth in me shall never die." And again, "I am come, a light in the world, that whosoever believeth on Me should not abide in darkness."

Is it any wonder the apostles got from all this the doctrine of "justification by faith?" Had Jesus not prayed for all that should believe on Him through the word of those very apostles? One does not feel at all surprised to find those early apostolic preachers of Christ asserting, as they did, with ceaseless and questionless fidelity, that without faith it is impossible to please God! Nor is it strange that the great Christian world ever since has held faith to be the vital thing on man's part in the gospel scheme; the appropriating act of the soul by which Jesus is accepted and embraced; the first in the order of the Christian graces; the hinge that turns the whole soul about; the trustful commitment of every interest for time and eternity to the Lamb of God, as the determining condition of everlasting life.

But recently it has been heralded with great blare of rhetorical trumpet and air of boastful confidence, that Matthew says nothing about faith.

The sufficient reply to this is: First, that even if this were absolutely true, no scheme is to be judged by one of its parts alone. Christianity, in its fullness and totality, is set forth in Christianity's book, not in a single chapter or section of it. Secondly, Matthew's words were written primarily for the Jews, to convince them that Jesus was the Messiah of Old Testament prophecy and promise, and to give them true views of the kingdom of God. The Jews did not need to have it insisted that they must believe in the Messiah when He came. They knew that. They were ready for that, or thought they were. What they did need was this—to be persuaded that Jesus was Himself the very Messiah predicted in their scriptures, and to be persuaded that the Messiah's kingdom was to be spiritual, over minds and hearts, and not the gross, carnal, material thing they were looking for. And the gospel by Matthew was designed to meet just this need. It exactly fits it all through. Third, though faith is not explicitly insisted on, it is fairly and fully and everywhere in Matthew most unmistakably implied. Listen: "Whosoever shall confess me before men, him will I confess also before my Father which is in heaven." That confession involves faith. "But whosoever will deny me, him will I deny." That denial involves unbelief. "Come unto me and I will give you rest." Come how, except by believing in him? "If any man will come after me, let him deny himself and take up his cross and follow me." But how can one do that and not believe? "Go and sell all that thou hast and give to the poor and come and follow me." Could a man do that and not believe utterly in him who bade him do it? " Go ye and teach all nations, baptizing them in the name of the Father, and of the Son and of the Holy Ghost." What is baptism but a sign and seal of faith. And what a farce to be baptized in the name of the Son, if we are not to " believe in the Son?"

But I need not further prick this bubble, blown out on the recent air and gilded with the hues of a brilliant but superficial rhetoric. You may count it quite certain, friends, that no confessed smatterer in critical exegesis has discovered, or is ever going to discover, a fatal objection to Christianity, where the ablest and most scholarly minds in the ranks of hostile criticism have searched in vain.

Mind you, I have not sought to show the reasonableness of faith in the gospel scheme; but that this very definite thing, salvation by faith, is indisputably in the gospel, and essential to what we call Christianity. Faith's place, and necessity, and reasonableness could easily be vindicated. Men stumble over it, and cavil at it, and have their sneers about it. But tell me if in every important relation of life it is not vital.

Distrust in the home makes a hell of it. Distrust in business makes a wreck of it. Distrust in government makes a mob of it. Distrust in God

makes a liar of Him. **How** can God possibly save
us while we practically say to His face, "I don't
believe you," i. e. save us in the gospel sense, by
taking us into His heaven, admitting us to His
confidence, privileging us with His fellowship, per-
mitting us to lean upon his bosom?

Now, object as men may to these truths and
doctrines, it cannot be gain-said that they constitute
Christianity. Say what they will about this
scheme of salvation, there can be no denying it is
the gospel scheme. And it contains some very
definite things—about God, about Christ, His person, His work, what He came for, God manifest
in the flesh, to seek and to save that which was lost—
to save from perishing; to save to everlasting life
out of an everlasting death; to save by the blood
of His cross, by His dying for us; and to save
through faith. These things are definite. These
things we know. These things are Christianity.
*Jesus Christ, the divine-human, Son of Man and
Son of God, God manifest in the flesh, a power
unto salvation from sin and endless death, by
atoning expiatory sacrifice through faith.*

If these things are truly embraced, out of them
will inevitably come a life—a life that will be a
constant struggle after the Christ-like; a ceaseless
and prayerful effort by the grace of God to attain

unto the measure of the stature of the fulness of Christ. If such life do not follow, the hope of salvation through Jesus Christ isn't worth a moment's cherishing. This we preach. For this, too, is Christianity. This defines and characterizes the faith. Faith without works is dead—the faith of devils, who believe and tremble. Faith that comes to blossom and fruit in Christ-like life, is of God. The life will be imperfect beyond a doubt. Christianity has never yet been lived perfectly on earth, except as Christianity's Christ may be said to have lived it. But men, millions of them, have tried to live it. Christianity has other and subordinate doctrines. And about these, men—good men, Christ-loving men—may differ. But they cannot differ about the great fundamental corner-stone truth of the gospel of God which I have named, and be Christians. They may be moral men, virtuous men, philanthropic men, men whose outward lives are more praiseworthy and lovable and unblamable than many who profess belief in the great truths of the Christian religion; but they are not Christians. Nor are all Christians who are enrolled on church registers. There are hypocrites in the church. There are persons self-deceived in the church. Christianity is not to be judged by these. Christianity is to be judged by those who believe in Jesus as their personal divine Savior, and *who try to imitate Him.* The church that preaches this and seeks in all her life to live it, that is the Christian church. There is sad and pressing need for such preaching. Over all our land men claiming to be Christ's heralds are preaching a mutilated, enervated, emasculated, forceless gospel. They are shading away its great, clear, sharply-defined truths, and making out of this glorious gospel of the blesssed God a gospel of impotence. O, let us understand that the power of Christianity lies not in a hazy indefiniteness, not in shadowy forms, not so much even in defi-nite truths and doctrines; but in *the* truth and *the* doctrine. There is but one, Christ crucified. All the gathered might of the infinite God is in that word.

V.

CHRISTIANITY'S VIEW OF MAN.

This is the state of man: to-day he puts forth
The tender leaves of hope, to-morrow blossoms
And bears his blushing honors thick upon him;
The third day comes a frost—a killing frost.
                              —SHAKSPEARE.

Thou pendulum betwixt a smile and tear.—BYRON.

The glory and scandal of the universe.—PASCAL.

What is man that thou art mindful of him?
                              —THE PSALMIST.

CHRISTIANITY'S VIEW OF MAN.

Who am I? Whence came I? Whither am I going? What is my being and character and destiny? What is man? These are questions asked in all ages. They are of unspeakable importance. To think seriously of what we are, may go far to make us think seriously and rightly of some other things, and to determine what we ought to do in view of them.

Christianity has a definite answer to this question, What is man? But before considering Christianity's view, let us see what man is, in the light of the facts of history and consciousness. If, then, the word of Scripture be found to answer to the facts—if it match all round and not only fit into the facts, but explain them and account for them, making dark things luminous and seeming contradictions easy of reconcilation, we shall have another buttress flung across in air to support our gospel temple walls. And if, moreover, we thus find a

wonderful adjustment of part to part in the great
gospel scheme, equation after equation, an infinite
need equaled by an infinite remedy, an immortal
ruin met by a divine Restorer, a power of endless
death answered to by a power of endless life, the
readier we shall be to take up the song of the
heavenly harpers and sing, "Great and marvelous
are Thy works, Lord God Almighty! just and
true are Thy ways, O King of saints!"

Let us see, therefore, what man is in the light of
nature.

The facts of consciousness and history disclose a
triple endowment of intellect, will, and affections.

Man thinks, reasons, is capable of logical pro-
cesses. Some of the lower animals appear to reason, but they never get very far in their lessons.
The bee and the beaver build with seeming fore-
thought and skill, in beautiful proportion and sym-
metry, but they build no better to-day than when
honey was first sucked from the flowers, and trees
were first felled by these native forest-choppers.
But man argues, establishes premises, passes from
premises to conclusions, makes premises of these,
and goes logically down, step by step, to other conclusions, and acts upon them constantly and without
fear. His intellect grows, too; has capacity for
expansion; arbitrates upon the several reports of

the senses; grasps, retains, accumulates, making past gains fruitful of gains still beyond and more precious.

Again, man chooses, wills, has a voluntary nature. He is subject to motives, weighs them, acts upon them. His external conduct may be compelled. His will cannot be. In the realm of choice his reign is absolute. Outward force may stop the purposed deed or indulgence, but the choice of the soul cannot be taken away, and against all opposition man may will on forever.

Still again, man has an emotional nature, is endowed with affections and passions. These are the springs and sources of his activity, the spur to the will. Sometimes, indeed, the will may push in lines of intense activity at the behest of the moral judgment, against a perfect clamor of the passions; but ordinarily the loves, joys, desires, hopes, and their like, are the stirrers to toil. Man loves and hates, desires and dreads, hopes and fears, by the very necessity of his being.

Embraced in this triple endowment of intellect, will, and affections, is *a moral sense*—a sense of oughtness and ought-not-ness—conscience. It is not so much an independent faculty as the entire inner spiritual being of man, acting in the realm of morals. It fixes obligation. It discriminates as to right and wrong. It impels or restrains. It punishes or rewards. It arises out of intelligence and voluntariness and the affectional nature, and conditions all responsibility.

This is man, as he is reported by consciousness— as he is seen in nature. This is that personal, conscious, inescapable I, which every living being knows of. I think, I will, I love. Something besides my body it is, that thinks and wills and loves. My body does not do these things. My body is not I.

Now let us go back and consider, first, the superb achievements of man's intellect. What great thoughts have been piled up through the centuries! What proofs they furnish of almost limitless power! "The great and wide sea" has been spoiled of its secrets, and its still, deep chambers are now made the passage-way of man's lightning-winged thought. The rock-ribbed continents have been compelled to tell the story of creation. Invisible scales have been flung out into space, and suspended there upon nothing, have weighed worlds. Listening intelligence has caught the notes of some unknown music amidst the heavenly harmonies, and pointing unerring finger in a certain direction into the depths of space, has said, "There some undiscovered planet is praising God;" and the telescopic eye of science, turning thitherward at the bidden hour, has discovered the stranger.

And wide as is the domain of knowledge, the area is being constantly enlarged. The out-posts of intelligence are being pushed farther each day, and the radius of human thought strikes each day a grander circumference. There is no known limit to the sweep of man's understanding.

Consider, secondly, the superb capabilities of man's will. No earthly force has ever yet been able to harness it to a beaten track of endeavor. It has never cared against what odds it battled. And it has won such triumphs that human resolution, in a burst of enthusiasm, has been pronounced omnipotent. Will to achieve or die; will to hold the mind to its task, even when the accomplishment of the task may be at the loss of reason; will to bear and smile when to bear at all is worse than death; will to force from hostile circumstances contributions to the will's influence and power; will to transform mountains into plains when they stand in the way of desire—this is the will of man. "There shall be no Alps" said Napoleon. And it was as if those cragged heights melted away before his imperial endeavor, so easily did he climb them at last by the famed roads he built.

Consider, now, thirdly, the sweep and power of

man's affections or passions. How love has possessed him, bowing his whole being, flaming out in heroic achievement and deeds of valor—in patient, unwearied, yea, joyful sufferance and martyrdom. How man has pitied, too, giving to mortals an almost infinite tenderness. And so divine has been the transformation in some of these ministering angels of mercy, that their very shadows have been kissed as gifts of God. What transformations hope has wrought, clothing poverty with purple, and making " palaces beautiful" of loathsome dungeons. What desires, also, are in man, forever beyond achievement. No heights have been high enough for his aspirations. Yearnings for knowledge, yearnings for light, yearnings for life and power, yearnings to be other than he is, as if there were some secret possibilities of his nature yet unlocked—how these have been mocked and baffled by poor accomplishment.

Such is man in his higher nature. Lodged in this physical framework are all these limitless capabilities of intellect, will, and affections. They crown man with glory and honor. They betoken a grand nature. They betray a grand origin.

But is the story all told when this is told? Is this the full answer to the question, What is man? By no means. Meanness and shame, as well as dignity and glory, attach to man. There are "gulfs of want" in his soul; rents and chasms and weaknesses and violences, justifying Pascal's portraiture: "A subject of contradiction" is man, "a confused chaos," "the great depository and guardian of truth, and yet a mere huddle of uncertainty"— "the glory and scandal of the universe!"

Let us go back over our ground once more, and see if this be not so. Take, first, man's intellect. While abating not one whit the splendor of this endowment, think of the insane follies upon which men have been bent, the strange and senseless theories that have been hugged and defended, the monstrous absurdities that have had endorsement, to the disgrace of reason. In what contradictions the famed intellects of the world have involved themselves. That contradictions may be true; that there is no such thing as matter; that there is no such thing as mind; that God is the universe, of which you and I, and the leaf on the highway, and the worm trodden under foot, are perishable bits; that there is no God—men have said all this. In the pride of their reason they have said it, and the very understandings producing such births have sometimes been those gifted the most and reaching farthest. When the Egyptians were the famed masters of all learning, they worshipped an ox, deified a cat, and adored to idolatry leeks and garlic. And over all the world for thousands of years men have repeated the stupidity and folly recorded in Isaiah, of those who hewed down a tree in the wood, and with one part of it made a fire, and with the residue thereof made a God. "As if," says South, "there was more divinity in one end of the stick than in the other." So Bacon has been called "the greatest, wisest, meanest of mankind." So the myriad-minded dramatist and poet was nevertheless an obscure and profane stage manager. So Napoleon, whose capacious head carried such trains of affairs, could listen at key-holes, and argue that he was beyond the possibility of crime because the child of destiny. Such are the shameful perversions and anomalies of reason along-side of its proofs of glory and power.

Think, too, of the spells and resurrections wrought by the imagination. Yet, what shame is linked with the glory of this faculty! What hideousness and deformity are in this realm of the beautiful. What contrast of angel-life and demon-life. What riot of evil in the chambers where man's holiest and heavenliest conceptions have had birth.

Pass now to man's will—the power of choice and purpose, lifting him out of the realm of mechanism and instinct and making him the conscious and independent arbiter of his own destiny.   And, alas! This high endowment is also his shame.   Man, in the exercise of his sovereign choice, has willed to do wrong; and· he has committed himself with a kind of imperial awfulness to evil endeavor.   His will-force has carried him across continents and through the ruins of states and kingdoms—counting men only as wretches to be hired and killed in the furtherance of his daring and determined purpose. And he has willed on, man has everywhere, against conviction and against conscience, against even the deepest longings of his soul— with unsatisfactoriness and unrest, with want and woe and weariness, he has willed on and willed to die so, rather than to yield his will to the will that makes for righteousness.

Turning to man's affections, scandal and shame here also hang out their signals.   These endowments might well be deemed the bond and cement of the race; but what jars, repugnances, transports of malice, violences of revenge, frenzies of remorse, swoops of unhallowed passion are here, often carrying the soul against will, against intellect, against conscience.   Love is frequently only a more cleanly name for lust.   Desires in man press and plunge him to depths of infamy as well as incite him to heights of glory. Hate, the very opposite of love, gleams out of men's eyes. Anger flushes and flashes in men's faces, and spends its swift bolt, oh! how often, in deeds of murder. Avarice binds man to his coffers with a self-denial that would be sublime in behalf of truth. This is the crazy mixture of the passions.

And amidst all this, what of the moral sense? Well, here too is dread perversion, and perhaps the darkest shame. Conscience is seared. The blackest crimes of history get endorsement. In good conscience mothers kill their sweet babes. In good conscience men ply the rack. In good conscience men stamp out the holiest instincts of the heart. Man is made a conscientious fiend.

Let me name one thing more that nature suggests, but does not assert, in answer to the question, What is man? That he is immortal, that somehow death does not end all. Nature gives no proof— no positive and absolute proof. But there are hints, suggestions, inferences, instincts, analogies, probabilities, that bring us almost to the very door of certainty.

The expectation of something beyond is in all breasts. And there must be something there—an unseen orb—to so draw all human souls. So men guessed in the dim past. So they looked out half

blindly into the future, ages ago, and vaguely believed. So they indefinitely reasoned at Athens.
So the soul's immateriality, and the soul's longings, and the soul's capabilities would seem to indicate. By these are intimated possibilities of development there is no room for in this earthly life.
And they seem to lift the frail and perishable creatures of a day out of the grasp of dissolution, and to
say with a mighty confidence, "Ye are, and can
not die." Shall he who has penetrated the arcana
of all nature, who has harnessed the lightnings, las-
soed unseen planets, traced the track of invisible
comets, conquered earth, and sea, and air, and made
everything in them tributary to himself, shall he
who has found nothing yet in this earthly existence
that meets and fills the broad expanse of his desires, who comes to death's door with unsatisfied
longings just as eager and mighty as those experienced anywhere this side death—shall he die as the
brute dieth, and be buried with the burial of an
ass?

Well, it can not be denied that these voices of
nature give us hints, presumptions, tremendous
probabilities in favor of a life beyond death as
against the blank of everlasting silence. Hence
man has everywhere believed, in all ages, and almost without exception, that man is immortal.

And yet here, too, what a contradiction he is! He wishes for a future life, and yet dreads it. All the currents of his being set full and deep against anni- hilation; he shrinks from it with a positive and al- most unconquerable aversion, and yet would wel- come annihilation rather than *be forever* as his haunting fears tell him he *may* be.

Such is man as nature shows him—a being of splendid powers—a being of contemptible powers —a being probably immortal—greatness, littleness, presumable everlastingness.

> "How poor, how rich, how abject, how august,
> How complicate, how wonderful,....
> Dim miniature of greatness absolute!
> An heir of glory! A frail child of dust!
> Helpless immortal! Insect infinite!
> A worm! A God!"

Now, does Christianity's answer to the question, "What is man?" match this, all round? Does it fit into these strange facts of history and conscious- ness?

I make bold to say it not only fits all the facts, but explains them, accounts for them, disposes of the seeming contradictions, solves the otherwise insoluble riddle, and pours a flood of light on man's dark and difficult case.

Christianity says, first of all, " God created man

in His own image—in the image of God created He him."

He was not made a thing, therefore, but a spirit —for God is a spirit. He was made a living intelligence, answering to the natural image of God. He stood Godlike amidst the finger-works of the Almighty, breath of divinity, a splendid creature, a living soul. He could know his Maker and talk with Him, for he was made after His image. He could think and choose and will and love, for God could do these, and he was Godlike. Between his heart and God's heart there was not a veil of filmiest gauze. Lovingly and holily they fellowshiped. There were no shifts, no violences, no disabilities. Love flamed up in fervors of devotion. Desire grew and was met as it grew in the wonders and glories of that divine communion. The will pushed out in right lines of activity, and to all heavenly behest was obedient and correspondent, while no thought was man's that God could not share.

Here is the source of those limitless capabilities of intellect, will and affections, which, we have seen, are possessed by man, and which crown him with glory and honor. The gifted creature is accounted for. No wonder he can think such thoughts; no wonder he is capable of such achievements; no wonder he is moved by such affections. He was made of God, in God's own image. This is Christianity's view of man, as he stood in his original estate—grandly endowed, a splendid being, divinely imaged, the consummate flower of creation.

But Christianity's further account of man is this: That he is a sinner—that he was tempted away from those original heights of communion and glory; that he broke from divine allegiance, and struck a blow at his own Creator. God had made him with the power of choice, and he chose to do wrong. God had made him with a will, and he refused to yield the leadership of his will to the will of God. He changed the glory of the uncorruptible God into an image made like to corruptible man, and he changed the truth of God into a lie, and he worshiped and served the creature more than the creator. He thus marred and defaced the moral image in which he was made. But he retained the natural image. He carried all his grand capacities with him in his fall—capacities of thought, and purpose, and passion. Man is intelligence and activity and affection still, as God is. But he is a spirit perverted—a will athwart God's will—an activity busy with sin, with all the dynamics of his original birthright put to the earning of sin's wages—a heart deceitful above all things, that no longer loves God, and desperately wicked.

Christianity holds, moreover, that this curse of sin has struck through man's whole nature, and left its unclean touch everywhere. Through and through all the realm of thought and feeling, in the domain of reason and the chambers of imagery, where the will thunders and the heart throbs, there is not a spot left holy, there is not a trace of that image of "righteousness and true holiness" in which man was originally made.

This is Christianity's view of man. And this matches the facts, and accounts for them. Man is a fallen principality—a being swung away from the glories of an original creation, but carrying with him all his deathless capabilities in his shame. Man is a ruin, but a ruin that betrays still the splendor of his past. Sin tells the story. Man was made like God, and he was not satisfied. He would be God. So he fell from his high estate. Therefore, the anomalies, and perversities, and contradictions of his nature; therefore, this glory and this shame, this greatness and this littleness; therefore, the exaltation and humiliation of reason; therefore, the will's mightiness in wrong; therefore, the "pendulum betwixt a smile and tear," the oscillating force between the deeps of degradation and the mountain tops of glory.

One thing more. Christianity says man is immortal. It comes with no guesses, analogies, probabilities. It comes with facts and living proofs. Outside of Christ there is nothing else concerning immortality but presumption. "But now is Christ risen from the dead." There once stood the eternal Son, in our body, on the way to die for us. And the great word on his lips was, "I am the resurrection and the life." Go, stand now by that open grave. Hear the angel saying, "He is not here. He is risen." Listen to the apostles as they get the meaning of the wondrous fact. "Blessed be the God and Father of our Lord Jesus Christ, who, according to his abundant mercy, hath begotten us again unto a lively hope by the resurrection of Jesus Christ from the dead!" We know now that death does not end all.

"Man is immortal," is the clear, ringing word of scripture. Immortal and guilty. A sinner, with lost God-likeness, and to be forever. Put these things together, and don't you see how again they exactly match the facts? Don't you see how it is that man wishes for a future life, and yet dreads it; shrinks from annihilation, yet welcomes it; clings to life even when getting no joy from it; and wants to die, yet dare not? Christianity's view of man accounts for these things. Nothing else does.

What is man? Christianity's answer is, Man is a ruin—a thinking ruin, the ruin of a divine image— the ruin of a deathless soul. He was made for God and made like God. But he is out with God. The harmony is broken. There is enmity between. There is discord in this realm. If God press His claims much, there is hate and open war. Meanwhile, man is drawn to God—drawn yet repelled. " O that I knew where I might find Him;" yet "whither shall I flee from His presence." There is discord in the domain of conscience, in the realm of the passions, in the seat of the will. How the altars have smoked around the world as men have sought God. How the air has been thick with blasphemies as men have denied God.

This great, awful, immortal ruin, who or what is to restore it? Philosophy cannot; for philosophy is born of the very ruin it would attempt to restore. So of every other device of human wisdom. Shall man come to his own rescue? Will you, my friend, undertake your own restoration? Where will you find fulcrum for the lever of your uplifting force? Where will you find lever for your force? Ah, where will you find force? You, yourself, are the ruin. Shall the ruin restore itself? Man is the ruin. Understanding, will, affections, body and soul, being and capacity of being, all are

smitten with the curse and ruin of sin. The woe
is too deep for human specific. Immortality can
not be swallowed up of mortality. The sinner
needs something for his recall and restoration more
potent than anything in or of the sinner. What
then? Must the ruin go on? Is there no eye to
pity and no arm to save? Listen to these blessed
words: "The Son of Man is come to seek and to
save that which is lost." Who is this Son of Man?
His name is called Wonderful, Counselor, the
mighty God, Immanuel, God with us, God manifest
in the flesh.

Now what have we found that Christianity
was—was and is? Jesus Christ, the divine-human,
Son of Man and Son of God, God manifest in the
flesh, a power unto salvation from sin and endless
death by atoning sacrifice through faith.

See, now, how the successive equations come out.
Is the need infinite? So is the remedy. Is it the
image of God that is so defaced? Then it is a
work worthy of God to restore the image. Did
God make man? Then there is fitness in God's
seeking to save. Was there divine wisdom in the
fashioning? There is divine wisdom in the re-
fashioning and redemption—wisdom bathed all
over with an infinite tenderness. Is it the power
of an endless death under which the ruin lies?

Jesus comes in the power of an endless life to seek and save.

Do you not see how part answers to part? Such a being, so fallen, and immortal—does it not justify this august and tender mission of Jesus Christ? Must not both be true—the need and the remedy, the ruin and the restoration, the endless death and the endless life? Sinner, sinner, you are the ruin; yours is the need; it is you who are under the power of an endless death. The ruin can not restore itself; there is no possible help for you, save through Jesus Christ; but if you will open the door of your heart and let Him in, yours will be the remedy and the restoration and the power of an endless life.

۲.

VI.

CHRISTIANITY NOT A FAILURE.

Look back to the cross, and the disciples gazing on it in terror from afar, and then look around on the nations that are influenced by the faith which there centres—and note the change! Then take these elements, established in history, and calculate the orbit Christianity is to fill.—STORRS.

Jesus is the purest among the mighty, the mightiest among the pure, who, with his pierced hand, has raised up empires from their foundations, turned the stream of history from its old channel, and still continues to rule and guide the ages.—RICHTER.

If this counsel or this work be of men it will come to naught; but if it be of God, ye cannot overthrow it.

—GAMALIEL.

The more we are mowed down, the more we spring up again. The blood of the Christians is seed.—TERTULLIAN.

CHRISTIANITY NOT A FAILURE.

Error is doomed. In the long run, it will go to the wall. The time comes for its exposure, and it is smitten to the death. ᛫ This is the common judgment of the world. This is the verdict of history. What is of God must be permanent, if it be in the shape of truth. What claims to be of God and is not, but is born of human device, will ere long be unmasked and its falsehood revealed. Christianity appeared in the person of its Founder over eighteen hundred years ago, and its great central truths had expression in the gracious words that proceeded out of His mouth. God was there, manifest in the flesh, a power unto salvation by atoning sacrifice. " Thou art the Christ, the Son of the living God," said Peter. " Upon this rock I will build my church," said Christ, " and the gates of hell shall not prevail against it." " There is none other name given under heaven among men whereby they can be saved." Heaven and earth shall pass away, but the word of the Son of the living God shall not pass away.

He, " being in the form of God, thought it not robbery to be equal with God, but made himself of no reputation and took upon him the form of a servant, and was made in the likeness of men; and being found in fashion as a man, he humbled himself and became obedient unto death, even the death of the cross.   Wherefore God hath highly exalted him, and given him a name which is above every name; that at the name of Jesus every knee should bow, of things in heaven and things in earth and things under the earth; and that every tongue should confess that Jesus Christ is Lord to the glory of God the Father."   That time is coming. Then there shall be great voices in heaven, saying: " The kingdoms of this world are become the kingdoms of our Lord and his Christ, and He shall reign for ever and ever."   Thus is Christianity down on record.   This is its proud and ambitious claim. It has entered upon the conquest of the world. And by its triumphs it means to vindicate the words of Gamaliel, that it is of God and cannot be overthrown.

But men are calling it a failure.   They say its work is virtually done, it is now a thing of the past—to be honored, indeed, for its instrumental agency in helping the race onward and upward, but outgrown and no longer serviceable.   They patronizingly speak of its virtues, just as they would speak of the virtues of the Jewish code, or of the Koran of Mohammed, or of the Veda of the Hindoos. They put the Bible on the same ground with the books of other religions. They take it just as they take these, accepting or rejecting as the fancy suits them. They don't believe in devils, nor in the " monstrous prodigies" of the gospels, nor in " teasing God, as an unjust judge into compliance with vain repetitions," which is a way they have of representing the doctrine of importunity in prayer; but they *do* believe and they say, that the Christian belief that Jesus was the Son of God "stands in the way of the human race and hinders our march."

This left handed way of complimenting the Christian religion clearly will not answer. This infidel stab at Christ is but another way of getting Him out of the world. Christianity is not something that has served the world very well during a certain state of its progress, but is now to be superseded. If it be that, all the eulogy in the world will not keep it from ranking as a failure and a fraud.

But it is not a failure? Were they dreamers of idle dreams who, in the time long since, sounded out the lofty prophecies of universal peace by the conquests of Christ, when all hate should come

under love's supremacy, and war should be no
more, and earth's angry noises should die in hushed
stillness at the door of God's temple, builded at
last for all the earth?   Are they apples of Sodom
that God's prophets have held to the lips of hope?
Or is it still true that the Christ born of Mary is to
be Prince of Peace at last, with the government
on His shoulder and the uttermost parts of the earth
for His possession?   Let us see what Christianity
has done, and what place it holds to-day, and what
is the fair promise for the future.   We shall thus
have the best answer to these questions.

You all know its origin, unquestioned now by
the most intelligent and most hostile skepticism.
Jesus Christ took twelve poor, illiterate men into
His company, kept them a brief while under His
instruction, went about with them, gained a few adherents to the new doctrine, commanded His disciples to go into all the world and make disciples of
all nations, and then left them.   With no equip-
ment save the truth their Lord had given them,
with no arms and no armies, no aid from the cabi-
nets of princes, no learning, no wealth, no power
of any kind, as men count power, providing neither
gold nor silver nor brass in their purses, they went
forth upon their strange undertaking.   They told
their story, they talked the word, they held up the

despised Nazarene, they said: " Believe and be saved; repent or perish. Idols are nothing; they are helpless to help you. Philosophy is vain. Your faith is not to stand in the wisdom of men, but in the power of God. We preach Christ crucified, to you Jews a stumbling-block, and to you Greeks foolishness, but nevertheless Christ, the power of God and the wisdom of God." Religion, custom, law, policy, pride, interest, vice, philosophy, letters, all were united against them.

The vast idolatry, embosomed in history, enshrined in art, having its home in song, a thing of the fireside, this arrayed itself against Christianity. The prevailing religions were indeed regarded by philosophers as false, but the masses believed in them and the powers of the state sustained them, and the laws were adjusted to them and upheld them. " Keep yourselves from idols," was the charge of these feeble disciples, and the command that Christianity flung into the face of heathendom. It would not and could not accommodate itself to the reigning superstitions, nor allow any association with them. " Why may you not still adore that God of yours in conjunction with our gods?" said a prefect of Egypt to Dionysius. "We worship no other God," was the unyielding reply. Such language was unpardonable in the ears of an idol worshiper. Yet Christianity held no other, built itself up only over the ruins of other systems, and ere long made all idols the outcasts of civilization. It swept away the heathen worship which was imbedded in the national rites and usages, authorized by the government, sanctioned by a rich and varied literature, supported by all the allurement of art, associated with the greatness and glory of the state, and thus wrought into the very life of the people.

The Jews, also, hated the new gospel, and arrayed themselves against it. They looked upon it as an apostasy from the religion of their fathers, a religion which was full of the tokens of Jehovah's presence and interlaced and interlocked with their most precious memories.

The philosophers, too, scorned with an utter scorn the humiliating doctrines of the cross, whose heralds came not with the enticing words of man's wisdom. Priests and people of all classes spurned it as a religion without a temple and without an altar. The imperial state lit the fires of persecution, loosed wild beasts, and flung the Christians as food to them, and tore assunder with the rack, to burn and kill out this hated thing, with its revolutionary and disorganizing tendencies.

Notwithstanding all this, Christianity spread,

multiplied its triumphs, without an army or a sword or a king, in poverty, in weakness as to numbers and learning, in spite of bigotry and violence, in spite of calumnies and persecutions, it moved steadily on, disrobing an established priesthood, overthrowing giant and defiant establishments, the growth of centuries, transforming pollution into purity and making multitudes of men great fearers of God, who yet had no fear of fire or famine or wild beasts. Martyrdom became their joy, and "the blood of the martyrs became the seed of the Church." In the hottest of the conflict they never shrank, says Cyprian, but maintained their ground with a free confession, an unshaken mind, a divine courage, destitute indeed of external weapons, but armed with the shield of faith. In torments they stood stronger than their tormentors; their bruised and mangled limbs proved too hard for the instruments with which their flesh was racked and pulled from them, and the blows, however often repeated, could not conquer their impregnable faith. Thus they preached and lived and died, until the truth shone everywhere, until Christ was known throughout Rome's vast empire, along all the borders of Spain, in the many countries of the Moors, in the different nations of Gaul, and even in those parts where the Romans did not reach; and at last

10

Christianity was the prevailing doctrine, and the kingdom of Christ was everywhere extended, and Rome's emperor himself became a disciple of Jesus.

I know it is said other religions, too, have spread, and found multitudes to embrace them. But they have not spread as Christianity, offering their converts nothing in the world but self-denial and sacrifice, and abasing the pride, crucifying the lusts, quelling the passions, demanding an utter self-surrender and a complete regeneration of the moral nature. The early Christians fought their way, fired by no passion save love, using no weapon save the word of God, sustained by no might save the might of faith, exhibiting no spirit save the patient forgiving spirit of Jesus. They subdued the world by dying for their religion. Surely Christianity was not a failure in the early centuries. And Gibbon's fifteenth chapter is an insult to intelligence.

But how about the centuries that followed? it is asked. What of Christianity in the so-called dark ages? Ah, it is true Christianity has been betrayed, corrupted, perverted from its high and holy ends and made to be the instrument of unutterable woes, even by its professed disciples. But even in these darkest and most adverse facts of Christian history, there is proof of the inherent and divine vitality of the religion of Jesus, and rightly regarded they furnish no support whatever to the assumption that Christianity is a failure.

Christianity had borne one test triumphantly. It had flung itself, as an infant of days, into conflict with an opposing world of idolatry. It had met the vigorous and combined assaults of Heathenism, Judaism, and imperial Rome, and had conquered. It had thus borne the test of the outward, and proved its power to cope with the ablest and wiliest external foes armed with every weapon that could be gotten from the armory of human craft and human rage. Could it bear the test of an inward assault? Could it pass through the ordeal of its own corruptions? Could it prove itself charged with a divine power of self-restoration, when debased and perverted by misbegotten opinions and unholy alliances and human errors? This was the question yet undecided. And the ages that followed these early triumphs settled it.

Constantine, swaying the proudest imperial sceptre, having become a believer in Christianity, must needs make it stronger by his regal patronage. He unites it to the state, allies it with the power of his imperial throne, lifts it to political place and prerogative, " which is the same as to say that he dooms it, for ages to come, to be the mother of all unholy arts and oppressions and the source of unspeakable miseries." Gregory the Great must have a consolidated church under the primacy of Peter, so that Christianity may be more stately and conspicuous by the pomp of a robed official and the paraphernalia of imposing forms. Then comes a supervision of Christianity, a taking it in charge, an attempt to mend it and improve it, until the ambitious supervisor of this heaven-born and divinely vitalized thing is inflated to a degree of pride that leads to the taking of God's own seat and the usurping of God's own prerogatives and the dispensing of God's own pardons. Then follows the overlaying and stifling of the pure gospel " by a mass of anti-Christian inventions and corrupt traditions." Celibacy and monastic retirement are recommended and rewarded, as the begetters of a higher spiritual life, thus making the disciples of Christ infidel to God-ordained society, and generating corruptions almost too monstrous to be believed. Images and pictures are set up in consecrated places as sensible representatives of spiritual truth, and alas, idolatry comes back again, reappearing in the very bosom of the church. Mary is thrust to a prominence even above her Lord, and glorious Christianity is transformed into " a fantastic scheme of Mariolatry." Bargains are made for indulgences, works are substituted for faith, sins are forgiven at a price.

Now can Christianity stand this unutterable and abominable perversion of her primitive purity of doctrine and life? Have these fearful corruptions and profligacies no power of death upon it? Can it exorcise the demoniac spirit of the hierarchy and throw off the subtle and monstrous errors therewith? This has been done. Christianity has proved equal to the task of purifying itself. The Reformation vindicated the power of Christianity to antidote by its own inherent and divine vitality the poison of internal corruptions. Meanwhile it had been proved by the Crusades that propagation by the sword is forbidden of God. Meanwhile, too, Christianity had been settling and compacting its true faith into abstract formulas and logical creeds. It came forth from the dark ages, thoroughly equipped, exorcised of its evil possessions, with no weapon for its warfare but the truth, took possession of the foremost nations, seized the printing-press just invented, and put it to publishing its glad tidings, crossed the sea to the new continent, and laid the foundation of its temples in the wilds of unbroken forests, and ever since it has been pushing its conquests, extending its domain, multiplying its victories, and scattering the leaves of the tree of life that are for the healing of the nations. It holds an influential place, and makes its power felt wherever learning, art, commerce, society, policy, and political dominion are the freest and the best. The leading civilizations of the earth to-day are Christian, not because their kings and emperors and presidents are Christians, nor because the name of God is in their constitutions, nor because their public documents recognize Christian obligations and express Christian beliefs, but because the common ideas and common beliefs and common tendencies and common consciences of these civilizations are Christian. The industry and intelligence of the ruling races, from which have been born commerce and trade, have been spiritualized and rendered saintly and heroic by Christianity. The great commercial states of antiquity had no such inner, spiritual, uplifting force. But those of to-day are indebted to it far more than is commonly believed. Ritter, in his "History of Philosophy," well says: "The great influence of Christianity would be less questioned if it had not penetrated so deeply and so widely into our being. We habitually bear about with us much that is exclusively Christian; which, however, having, as it were, become a second nature, is no longer looked upon as in any way an influence of Christianity, but is re-

garded as an ordinary element of man's character."
Our ideas concerning the treatment of idiots and
the insane, the deaf and dumb, and blind, are born
of Christianity. The very best men among the
millions of ancient heathendom would have laughed
at the suggestion of schools and asylums for the
training and care of mutes and maniacs and inebri-
ates. Christianity, too, has mitigated the horrors
of war, broken the power of tyranny, elevated the
masses, spread abroad what is the worthiest and
best in our notion of liberty.

Christianity has most near and vital relations to
education, to literature and to civil freedom.

To education. The Reformation was something
more than a protest against the corruptions of the pa-
pacy. It was a plea for the right of private judgment. And for the intelligent exercise of that right
there is a necessity for education. Hence, under
the direction of Luther, schools sprang up all over
Germany. Hence, wherever Christianity in its
purified form spread, the cause of general education was given a wonderful impetus. Zeal for religion, conspired with love of learning. Oxford
and Cambridge and the celebrated schools and colleges of Scotland were established and fostered by
the friends of Christianity. Within thirty years
after the landing of the pilgrims, they had laid the

foundations of our entire educational system. Our own colleges, in large part, had a Christian foundation. Just as soon as our forefathers had provided comfortable homes for themselves, and selected convenient places for the worship of God, they sought to found institutions of learning for Christ and the church. *Pro Christo et ecclesia*, is to this day the unchanged motto of Harvard college, though alas, its present spirit and life and influence belie the words. Yale college originated in a sincere desire to uphold the Protestant religion by securing a succession of learned and orthodox men. Princeton college was founded by the synod of New York. Dartmouth was established in the most elevated principles of Christian piety. Amherst college grew out of a charity-school; it was born of the prayers and baptized with the tears of holy men. So were scores of others throughout our land. State policy, state patronage, exclusive of religious influence, can not show a half-dozen flourishing colleges across the continent. Infidelity can not show one.

So, too, with literature. Christianity has a literature of its own, having given to the world some of its choicest treasures in this department. Calvin with the French, Luther with the German, Wycliffe with the Saxon, have done more than all others to preserve the purity of their respective tongues. And thus the three chief living languages of the globe are indebted to Christianity for their best forms of speech.

So, too, with liberty. Luther's ninety-five theses were so many blows at all institutional authority demanding blind assent and unreasoning obedience. The right of private judgment is the foe of despotism, whether ecclesiastical or political. It swept men out into a larger and larger freedom. The gospel is a charter of liberty, equality, and fraternity. It is the greatest leveler the world knows. It opposes all caste. It took its place in mens' hearts, in the bosom of society, and it did its leavening work. It regenerated the laws and political liberties of the English nation. Hume, who cannot be charged with favoring Christianity, says: "England owes whatever of civil liberty it enjoys to the influence of the Puritans." Christianity came to our shores, and here laid the foundations of that freedom which is to-day our glory and our pride.

But these are only the minor relations of Christianity—its secondary and subordinate effects. It is as a power unto salvation, changing men's minds, transforming their natures, purifying their hearts, that it claims to be sent of God. And here certainly, it is no failure.   It is doing to-day just what it has always done, changing vice into virtue, pollution into purity, hate into love, revenge into forgiveness, lawlessness into obedience.   There are personal exemplifications of its transforming power occurring all over our land and world.   On the coasts of Africa those who once were slaves to lust now delight in purity—those who once hated and murdered each other now pray for their enemies.   "By the grace of God," say these new-born souls, "we are what we are."   It is not commerce, nor philosophy, nor letters, that is humanizing them, uplifting them, changing the savages into saints, and woman, a slave, a beast of burden, a victim of lust, into woman, the queen of a home hallowed and peaceful—it is the gospel of the blessed God.   At the Hawaiian islands it has changed in a half century the character, habits, and moral life of a nation.   The captain of the little brig Thaddeus, that bore the first missionary party there, had permission of the ship-owners to bring back the poor creatures when they should realize the folly of their enterprise.   But it has well been said there was one on board the Thaddeus whose name was not down on the ship's register.   Not with powder and ball and shot and shell, but with the living word of God did they go forth to conquer those islands for Christ, and they conquered them. There they are to-day, morally and spiritually revolution-ized. The superstitions and degradations of heathenism, although the more debased and cor-rupted by contact with the civilized world, have been supplanted by the usages and institutions of a Christian nation. The thing that has done this— is it not of God? And can it, with any regard to truth, be termed a failure?

Mohammedanism, the religion of the false pro-phet, did indeed once enter upon a career of con-quest, and it lodged itself as a faith in the hearts of great peoples, but it did it " by the fierce apostleship of arms," by appeals to lust, by pandering to pas-sion. What there is really noble in it was borrowed or stolen from Christianity, and the rest is only a gratification of the natural selfishness of the human heart. Christianity's conquests are all peaceful; by the word, not by the sword; by love, not by power. But it makes no truce with human selfishness; extends no indulgences to sin. It de-mands the crucifixion of the old nature—a complete renunciation of every way of evil. It goes directly into conflict with sinful nature; and self-sacrifice is the very law of its life.

Other religions flow with the current of man's nature, and if they have had a permanence and a prevalence in the world, it is no wonder, even as it is no wonder that the waters of Niagara keep on over the rapids for thousands of years. Why not, with nothing to oppose them? But Christianity breasts the current—goes upward steadily, making progress against that hell of disorder and disability begotten of sin in our world. " Christianity rises and raises its adherent races with it." False religions die, as their adherent races die. Christianity, again, has already proved its power to subdue all races—every people and kindred, and tribe and tongue. It has universal adaptability. It sweeps, too, the scale of mind, triumphing everywhere, from the highest to the lowest, commanding the homage of the loftiest intellects, and yet furnishing food for those who are scarcely distinguishable from the mindless brute. Here Newton and Locke and hosts of others bowed and believed. Here Milton bathed his wings. And here many a little child and many an ignorant savage have entered into the joy of their Lord.

The great founders and law-givers in the world of philosophy—where are their schools to-day? Plato, with his deeply-cultured soul, embodied his wisdom, his mighty and beautiful thought, in a book. But what has his " Phaedo " done for the world? An Emerson indeed says: " Burn your libraries, for they are all in this book. Buddhism is in it, Mohammedanism is in it, Christianity is in it." But men do not burn their libraries. They know that infidel cry is rhapsodical nonsense. They do not read Plato much. But millions to-day study with deepest reverence the words of the unlettered mechanic. And the doctrine and life of Jesus are expounded and unfolded by the richest learning of the world.

Yet there are men saying with an air of great confidence that the days of Christianity are numbered. Only this last week I was addressed after this fashion: " It must be quite evident to you that evangelical Christianity is losing ground rapidly. And I predict to you now that it will continue to lose ground in an accelerated ratio from year to year."

This, in view of the fact that far more homes than ever before in any year of our Lord have just celebrated Christmas! This, in view of the fact that never before since Christ were so many millions week by week studying the gospels, with helps multiplied and perfected by the best learning of our time, old and young finding their profit and their joy in getting at the treasures of Bible truth! This, in view of the fact that modern Christian missions are the birth of this century, are scarcely fifty years old, and yet are to-day being prosecuted with a vigor and learning, and hope, and mastery of the world's languages simply marvelous, encircling continents and piercing their pagan darkness, and preparing to cross and recross their wide moral wastes, and expecting to triumph everywhere in Christ Jesus.

Christianity a failure! Then man is a failure. Then the race is a failure. Then the government of God is a failure. The man whose face is seamed and ridged all over with the fruits of vice says virtue is a failure. The bloated, besotted, driveling inebriate says temperance is a failure. The highwayman and the murderer say law is a failure. The reckless violaters of the laws of health say the science of medicine is a failure. Pope Pius IX. said the civilization of the nineteenth century is a failure. The owl says light is a failure. Is it any wonder that men may be heard to say Christianity is a failure? It's an old cry. Every single century since Christ it has been sounded out. But somehow this thing we call Christianity does not fail. Meanwhile, of exploded scientific theories that had their brief day and then were snuffed out, what a long roll can be called. And the charge of Christianity's failure never seemed quite so absurd as in the high noon of this nineteenth century. He only can make the charge who shuts his eyes to some tremendous facts, and who is smitten with the notion that his own little world of doubt and cavil is the whole wide world of thought and feeling of to-day.

Let it be frankly confessed that Christian discipleship might be improved. Undoubtedly there are tares in the wheat. Beyond question if the fires of persecution were kindled again, as they were in the early centuries, there would be some professed fearers of God who would be found to be greater fearers of them that kill the body; and the church of Christ would have some winnowing. There would be Luthers and Cranmers and Husses, Peters and Pauls and Stephens, a goodly and glorious company, without a doubt. But some, it is to be feared, would hide their light under a bushel, rather than make light by their quivering, burning flesh.

Let it be confessed, also, that wider conquests might have been achieved for Christ; that better and richer results might have been, and ought to have been, produced by Christianity's net-work of missions. If we count men, the majority are still anti-Christian. But the foremost nations are nominally Christian. In all the leading civilizations there is no power like Christ, the power of God. No person on earth, or that ever lived on earth, is so much talked about, and written about, and thought about this very hour as Christianity's Christ. No volume of literature, nor any collection of volumes, nor all literature combined, stimulates such thought, kindles such hopes this very hour as Christianity's book. The mightiest currents of feeling now flowing through the world have their source in the crucified Galilean. Christianity, to-day, lights up the earth as the beautiful feet of morning upon the mountains, and the dark places of cruelty and barbarism are where its beams have not fallen. Wherever its banner is uplifted there are signs of progress. It is pushing its outposts steadily farther and farther into the region and shadow of death. It hesitates not to grapple with the hoariest iniquities. It dares fling its forces into the very heart of heathendom. Forces! It has none, save its word, Christ crucified, and faith in that word. But these it thinks enough for the conquest of continents. And so it is constantly and everywhere aggressive.

It rests content with no past achievement—is satisfied with no fresh victories, however glorious and mighty. It hangs out no signals of decay; exhibits no marks of growing impotency; abates neither hope nor heart. Men everywhere, of high degree and low degree, learned and ignorant, continue to believe it, yield to it, bow at the foot of its uplifted cross. From the east and from the west, and from the north and from the south, they come, and the numbers increase as they come, to worship the Christ of God. The tokens of universal triumph grow brighter and brighter. Hail, millenial day! Speed thy coming, oh, thou time of prophecy and promise. Come, Lord Jesus; come quickly.

Meanwhile, if there be one thinking something like this, " Well, if Christianity be a success, if all things are possible with it, why am I not a Christian? Certainly, so far as I am concerned, it is a failure;" let me urge you to stop and think a little more deeply. What if the trouble be with you, and not with Christianity? Is the physician a failure, if you grow worse under his care, because you do not mind his directions? Is the barometer a failure, because the sailor does not mind its warnings? Is Christianity a failure, because the sinner freely and deliberately rejects its claims and its offered terms of mercy? You see, there are two sides to this question. My friend, you may be a failure—an eternal failure. And the saddest of all failures is that of a soul, with its capabilities and possibilities, failing of life everlasting, and entering upon that night of death upon which morning never dawns. Oh, let Christ in, and give Him room in your worldly

11

heart, so that He may be to you as He has been to so many millions, neither a stumbling-block, nor foolishness, but the power of God and the wisdom of God.

VII.

CHRISTIANITY AND ENDLESS DEATH.

It had been good for that man if he had not been born.
—JESUS CHRIST.

Which way I fly is hell.   Myself am hell.
—SATAN, in MILTON's *Paradise Lost*.

We must not let go manifest truths because we cannot answer all questions about them.--JERERMY COLLIER.

And these shall go away into everlasting punishment. —JESUS CHRIST.

CHRISTIANITY AND ENDLESS DEATH.

There are two standard objections brought against Christianity. One is brought against its doctrine of forgiveness; the other against its doctrine of punishment. Its doctrine of forgiveness is regarded as pushing forbearance to the limit of cowardice and pusillanimity. The doctrine of punishment, as almost universally interpreted, is regarded as making God harsh, hard, unjust, a tyrant. Men are thus too just for its mercy, and too merciful for its justice. When it comes to the treatment of their enemies its inculcations are altogether too lax, implying weakness and imbecility. When it comes to the treatment of God's enemies its threatening are altogether too severe, implying harshness and cruelty.

The most natural reply to these objections is that they neutralize each other. If we are asked to forgive men as God forgives us, and we can not do it and will not do it; if we demand that repeated and stinging and causeless provocation be punished, with no love in our hearts for the wrong-doer and no willingness in our hearts to bless him, and no disposition in our hearts to overcome his evil with our good; and God says there is all this in His heart toward all men, even though constant and flagrant and infamous in their treatment of Him— then what becomes of our assumption that we are more merciful than God because He declares that the wages of sin is death, and that He will by no means clear the finally guilty?

Another reply to this arraignment of God's justice is that it would be a poor principle in criminal jurisprudence to allow the criminal to affix penalty to crime. Suppose thieves were allowed to make laws for theft! Would you let a common murderer, who cared no more for human life than for the life of a dog, determine the penalty for murder? What great guilt can a man see in spoiling virtue who has not one instinct of virtue? Well, is the violator of the law of God in any better condition to decide the penalty due that violation? Remember, sin blinds; sin hardens; sin blunts the keen edge of moral sensibility; sin sears the conscience, perverts the judgment, biases the will. Shall the sinner, in love with sin, habituated to sin, frame a measure of his guilt out of his own consciousness? Is he the one to fix the penalty of his own transgression?

Still, again: What creature has climbed God's heights? Who, but God himself, knows all the relations and bearings of obedience to God? Who is aware of the infinite and eternal interests that possibly hang on the very law whose violation the sinner is guilty of every day and hour of his life? Who knows the reason and reach of that law, the tremendous concerns it guards, the necessities of its dread sanctions, that he can speak with such positiveness of the injustice of its penalty. God's government is one of law. Law without penalty makes government a farce. Penalty must be commensurate with the interests involved.

But it is said, no *man* would punish another forever, for the sins of a lifetime. God will not. He is not harder and harsher than His creature. Letting men eternally perish is not what man would do, and hence the doctrine cannot be true of God. A man, though his past life has been bad, who does a heroic deed and dies doing it, isn't going to hell, scripture or no scripture. No loving human heart would send him there. And surely not the loving heart of God.

> " Christ ain't a-going to be too hard
> On a man that died for men."

There it is, as it crops out in the concluding lines

of one of John Hay's Pike county ballads. It is a prevalent sentiment.

But who art thou, O man, that repliest against God? Hast thou the sweep of the universe, and knowest thou the reasons of the Almighty, that thou decidest what, in His infinite wisdom and love, God will and can do, and what He will not and can not? Are God's ways to be measured by man's? Well, then, look at Chicago before the great fire. What prodigious labor was here, what vast expenditure, what vital connection with material values the world over, what happy homes!. And, then, how swift and utter the desolation. How the hot flames went leaping and dancing over the doomed city in demoniacal delight, laughing at the tired firemen, flinging themselves after the panic-stricken crowd, as if in remorseless rage, scorching and consuming human flesh, making a hundred thousand homeless, and weighting many lives with a sorrow whose shadows fall yet. Recall the acres of ashes and blackened ruins, the charred corpses, the hopelessness, the bitter, bitter tears, the anguish, anxieties, apprehensions, fears, disturbances, and actual sufferings that stretched from that fire around the world. Would you do that, or allow it? God did. Look at that gaunt crew on that storm-swept, dismantled vessel, thinned down so that a mother would scarce know her boy among the skeletons, dying by slow starvation, and one of them scribbling in the last delirium of hunger on a bit of paper that he puts in a bottle but has not strength to cast into the sea: " Lord Jesus, guide this to some helper. Merciful God, don't let us perish,"—and getting no answer. Would you do that, or allow it, if you had the management of the world? God does. Think of the pestilences, producing horrors on which imagination dare not dwell; think of the famines, where men and women and prattling babes die in prolonged and frightful agony; think of the mean, base, dastardly men that place their heels of usurped and lawless power on the neck of innocence and virtue, while truth is dragged in the street and made to bite the dust amidst the derisive shouts and blasphemous orgies of the emissaries of the prince of the power of the air celebrating their hellish victories! Would you allow this if the reins were in your hands? God does. Ah, no man knows what he would do if he were in God's place, and could see as God sees.

Are we not forced to admit that God may have infinitely wise and satisfying reasons for what appears harsh and hard in His works and word? We must either come to this, or come to charge

God openly with injustice, or come to atheism.
Either the God of the Bible is the God of the universe and good in both, or the God of the Bible is
the God of the universe and bad in both, or there
is no God at all.

But men do not take easily to the absolute denial
of God.   There is something morally and mentally
monstrous in atheism.   Nor do they take easily to
shaking their fists in the face of the Almighty and
arraigning Him as a tyrant.   So rather than get
rid of God, and rather than defy God, they will go
to God's truth *to get the kind of God they want.*
Hence the challenge of the doctrine of eternal punishment.   Men do not wish it in the Scriptures.
They look to see if it is really there.   Most men
find it there.   Against all the instincts of the heart,
against some of the deepest feelings by which man
is moved, they find it nevertheless.   Only the merest inconsiderable fragment of the Christian scholarship of all the world in all ages has failed to find
it.

But a few have not read it in these Scriptures.
Some, in the sympathy of their hearts, have not
read it here.   Some, with a superficial investigation, have not read it here.   Some, with a wild
desire to get rid of its eternal sanction, have not
read it here.   Some have exhausted language in

picturing the material awfulness of a literal lake of
fire eternally blistering, and scorching, and consuming the lost, and then have shouted: "Away with
this doctrine of eternal punishment."   But the great
body of humble Christian believers and the great
body of profound Christian scholars hear what
these men have to say in advocacy of "universal
salvation," or "conditional immortality," or "eternal hope," and they go back to their Bibles, and
still they read, even as before, the doctrine of eternal punishment.   Tell me why.   They do not want
to read it so.   Millions of as tender hearts as there
are in this world find it in their Bibles.   The vast
majority of Christian scholars, age after age, search
these Scriptures with the possibility before them of
some other conclusion, and still they find it.   Why?
There is only one answer.   They find it because
it is there.   They believe it because they must.

And now, to clear the fog that has enveloped
this doctrine in the lowlands of unbelief, to free it
from the gross misrepresentations of hate and the
erroneous inferences of ignorance, let me, as briefly
as possible, state Christianity's true relation to the
punishment of the other world.

1. Christianity reveals the punishment.   It
does not make it.   It is uncovered by Christianity,
brought to light.   Conscience tells men the world

over that they are guilty, and that they will be
punished for their guilt. Christianity simply
makes this fact more clear, throws light on that
future track of doom, sets forth the exact truth
about the matter. The gospel does not coin the
punishment or make the sinner. Men are sinners,
and there the punishment is. Hell, therefore, has
not been built by Christianity. There is a hell,
Christianity or no Christianity. Does the headlight of the locomotive make the jaws of death into
which the express train plunges because of some
misplaced switch? The dread doom is there, and
the headlight only tells the engineer he is swiftly
approaching it Too late, often, the telling is, for
saving. But Christianity's light, shot clear ahead
on the pathway of the sinner, is never too late, if
heeded. It is given expressly for warning and rescue.

2. Christianity shows the punishment to be of
different degrees. It says, unto whomsoever much
is given of him shall much be required. It says, it
shall be more tolerable for wicked cities, like
Sodom and Gomorrah, in the day of judgment,
than for cities with far greater privileges, and those
privileges unimproved. It says, those sinning without a knowledge of God's written law will not be
judged by that written law, but only by such law

as is written in their hearts.   The punishment is to be exactly according to the sin, as determined by the light and the opportunity of each sinner.

So the punishment of a heathen, groping in darkness, will be far different from, and far less than, the punishment of a rejecter of Christianity in the full blaze of the gospel.   The punishment of one reared in a home of vice, never hearing the name of God but in blasphemy, taught by surrounding example only foulness and falsehood, will be far different from, and immeasurably less than, the punishment of one to whom religious instruction, pious example, a father's counsels, and a mother's prayers have been given in vain.

3. Christianity uses material images to represent this punishment.   It represents the future abode of the finally impenitent as an "abyss," a "bottomless pit," a "lake that burneth with fire and brimstone," a Gehenna "where the worm dieth not and the fire is not quenched," as a place of "outer darkness," a "place of torture," and by other such tremendous images.   These quotations, mind you, are not from Jonathan Edwards, or Dante, or Milton, but from Jesus and from His beloved disciples. Of course they are figurative.   They can not be literally understood.   There can be no literal lake of fire, for then there would be no undying worm and

no bottomless pit. It is a spiritual world that lies beyond death, and the punishment is largely spiritual. It is the conscious soul that will suffer, through conscience, and memory, and revelation of the righteous judgment of God. They are figures of speech, therefore, by which Christianity represents future punishment. But what terrible figures they are—the most significant, most impressive, most awful in human language. As if it were impossible by any figure to represent too vividly the anguish of the mind! What are physical tortures compared with the agonies of a wrathful conscience? "The mind is its own place, and can itself be hell."

4. Christianity represents this future punishment as endless. It lifts no flag of eternal hope anywhere over the future world. It reveals no point along the path of future punishment where the punishment shall end in annihilation. In proof of this I shall not enter into the discussion of the exact equivalent for the Greek word translated "everlasting" or "eternal" throughout the New Testament. I have no doubt of its meaning, as applied to the future state, of either the saved or the lost. But I prefer now another line of discussion.

Take, first, the unmistakable trend of the teachings of Jesus, and see if the irrevocableness and

finality of His words concerning the dead that die
in their sin, do not put it past all doubt that hope
forever ends with the impenitent when life ends.

He spake the parable of " the tares " and of " the
net," and then put His own interpretation on them,
saying, "So shall it be at the end of this world; the
angels shall sever the wicked from among the just,
and shall cast them into the furnace of fire." He
said there would be at the last those applying
for admittance to heaven, to whom He would say,
" I never knew you. Depart from Me." And,
again, "Depart from Me, ye cursed, into everlasting fire." He put those brief but terrible words,
" The door was shut," into the parable of the ten
virgins, as if there would come a time with some
souls when it would be forever " too late." He
said of those who should be invited, and who
should finally refuse to come to the gospel feast:
" None of those which were bidden shall taste of
My supper." And yet are they to taste of it after
all? He asked certain men how they could escape
the damnation of hell. And He said that at that
great judgment scene which He Himself pictured,
and where He Himself should be the judge,
"There will be gathered all nations, and there will
be one great separation of the righteous and the
wicked. The wicked on the left shall go away into

everlasting punishment, and the righteous on the right into life eternal." He lifts the veil once again, and distinctly tells us that they who would pass from that place of torment to that abode of the righteous, can not, for between the two there is a great gulf fixed. Here are two ways, two destinations, two futures, two certanties, two eternal realities, two conditions of endless existence, and only two, for all the world, clearly set before us by Him whom all Christians, infidels, materialists, moralists, scientists now unite to honor for His matchless tenderness and world-wide charity, and whose life is confessedly the loveliest ever lived among men. And this same Jesus says again and again that the one only thing which is to determine which of these two eternal futures is to be the future of each soul hearing His gospel is the penitent and believing acceptance of this gospel, or its continued and willful rejection. He says the Son of Man, meaning Himself, is lifted up on the cross that whosoever believeth in Him should not perish, but have eternal life. He says, " God so loved the world that He gave His only begotten Son that whosoever believeth in Him should not perish, but have everlasting life." He says, again: " This is the will of Him that sent me, that everyone that believeth in Me may have everlasting life." Of like import are His solemn words: " Ye will not come to Me that ye might have life. Except ye repent ye shall all likewise perish. Except a man be born again he can not see the kingdom of God." Here it is, then, by Christ Himself—not by some stern herald of wrath, but by the being whose life and teachings have done more to make men love each other than all other influences in the world. There is, in all the Bible, no such terrific imagery of spiritual and endless death as His, and He certainly knows whether there is such a death for the soul. What does He say about it? He calls it a damnation, a wailing and gnashing of teeth, a hellfire, a torment, an everlasting punishment. It is true, as I have already said, that some of these are figurative terms, but if you range through the whole compass of human language you will find no words that can convey to the mind more impressive and mighty sense of the profound and awful reality of this death of the soul.

There is another way of ordering this matter in our struggle after a possible conception that shall bring the realities of this truth in any impressive measure before us.

What think ye of Christ? Who was He? Do you believe Him to be what these Scriptures declare—God manifest in the flesh? Who is God?

12

Is He not a being infinite, eternal, and unchangeable in His wisdom, power, holiness, justice, goodness, and truth? He created the heavens and the earth. He appointed the stars their courses. He spangled infinite space with blazing suns. To whom will ye liken God? It is He that sitteth upon the circle of the earth, and the inhabitants thereof are as grasshoppers? He weigheth the mountains in scales and the hills in a balance. To him a thousand years are as one day, and whole nations as a drop in the bucket. How can we measure the being of whom such things can be said? Who, by searching, can find out God? Yet whither shall we flee from His presence? The everlasting God, the Lord, the Creator of the ends of the earth, holy, and just, and good, infinite in majesty and power, the august and mighty Jehovah, maker of all worlds and all beings of all worlds, breathing into man's nostrils the breath of life, so that he became a living soul, as able to speak this world out of existence as He was to speak it into existence, from everlasting to everlasting, the same yesterday, to-day, and forever, an invisible, everywhere present, all-wise, almighty Spirit—this is God. And Jesus was this God, God manifest in the flesh. He did the works of God and proved His power. He spake the words of God and proved His wisdom. What is this divine being here for? What has this great God come into His own world to do? Why has He taken the form of a servant and consented to the fashion of a man? God is in His own world and has not where to lay His head. Myriads of angels would be swift to do Him honor, and would count a smile from Him glory enough for eternity; but the men He has made turn their backs on Him and treat Him with open scorn. He submits to their insults. When He is reviled He meekly bears the reviling, and lets no lightnings blast the impious lips. And at last He, the God of the universe, whose throne is in the highest heavens, the God manifest in the flesh, allows Himself to be seized, to be tried in cruel mockery, to be unjustly accused of treason,—He, the King of kings,—to be crowned with thorns, to be led away in the midst of a rabble to a place of skulls and there nailed to a cursed tree and scoffed and jeered at until He is dead.

I want you to think now why He did all that. Did He do it all for nothing? Certainly He did if it makes no difference whether men accept Jesus Christ or reject Him. He says He did it to seek and to save that which was lost. He says He did it that whosoever believeth in Him might not perish. And if to perish and to be lost mean what the Son of God says they mean, if hell is the place of eternal despair and death that His terrible imagery represents it to be, then there was some reason for His coming. I can see how even God might be led to manifest Himself in the flesh, in a world where deathless souls were going down to the doom of eternal death, and how even He might rear a cross in that world and die on it, so as to save those souls. And He has done just this, the eternal God in Jesus Christ. Nothing but a work of infinite consequence would have brought Him from the skies. He saw all the realities of woe involved in the death of the soul, and He came for rescue. The cross and passion of the Son of God crowd a world of anguish into such a death. They tell us, as no words can, that it is an awful thing to die in one's sins. They reveal an awfulness and dreadfulness of death as the wages of sin that you can not find in the most vivid and intense language descriptive of the state of the lost.

There is still another way of ordering this matter. Think of heaven itself. Let us turn our minds to that other world, the home of another order of beings—" an innumerable company "—the angels of God. John saw them round about the throne, ten thousand times ten thousand and thousands of thousands. They are called a great host—God's host. These angelic hosts are said to excel in strength, to have great power, to be swift of passage. They are occupied in doing God's commandments, announcing God's law, conveying God's messages, protecting God's people, inflicting God's penalties, sharing in God's counsels, sounding God's praises. Theirs is a world of light and joy unspeakable, and full of glory. They are a high and privileged order of sinless intelligences, who kept their first estate,—unfallen spirits reflecting the glory of their God.

Are they interested in our world? We are told they are. What is it that interests them? He who came from God, and went to God, and who was God, and whom all the angels of God worship— He tells us there is joy in the presence of the angels of God over one sinner that repenteth.

What joy there was in the cities of the north after Gettysburg, when it was felt that Philadelphia and Pittsburg were safe. What joy stirred all loyal hearts when the news came of the fall of Richmond, and it was felt that the country was safe. What tearful, thankful joy in individual homes when, after a bloody battle, the wires flashed the glad tidings: " Thank God, father, mother, your boy is safe!"

But here is a joy that stirs a whole world—a

world of beings far away, superior to us, occupied with other interests, God's angels, an innumerable company, filled to the full with the satisfying delights of the service and the worship of heaven, bathed and bathing in the ineffable glory of the kingdom of God; and the occasion of their joy, the incident that stirs and thrills them, is the repentance of a single sinner in this sinful world. Every time one sinner turns from the error of his ways a tide of joy sweeps through all the hosts of heaven. "Saved," is the glad shout, "a soul saved from death." If the death is nothing, then the salvation is nothing, and the joy is a mockery, a farce—there is no joy. No whole world, distant, and glorious, and peopled with hosts of high intelligence, can be stirred with joy for nothing. I tell you the soul's death must be everything conceivable—yea, it must be with realities utterly inconceivable, or all heaven would not be moved with joy every time a soul is saved. Terrible must be the realities and powers of an endless death for the tidings of one poor sinner's escape to produce such an effect. Look, therefore, which way we will, whether at the direct scriptural statements of death as the penalty of sin, or at the agony of the cross as a means of rescue, or at the joy of the angels of God over a rescue; we see from either that it must be a work of infinite and eternal consequence—this work of redemption. To save a soul is to save it from a death to which the words of the Bible, and the passion of the cross, and the joy of the angels alike give a world of woeful meaning. Disciple of Jesus Christ, have you done such a work? Have you honestly, heartily, prayerfully, looking to God for help, directly and personally attempted to do it? Have you ever used all the means within your power to save one single soul? Have you ever sat down deliberately to think and study and plan and devise how you could best reach and influence, by what possible agency or instrumentality you could directly persuade an acquaintance, a friend, a scholar, a child, an associate, to come to Jesus? Is it not worth the while of every disciple of Christ to be doing this thing? Do you believe in this terrible death of the soul? Do you believe there are persons in your own pew, in your own family, in your own class, in your own place of business, who are in peril of this death? If they were in peril of bodily death, and were going on heedless of the peril, blind to it, or careless concerning it, would you stand on ceremony? Would you wait long to warn them? Would not your love and anxiety make a way of reaching them? But what is the death of the body to this other and second death of which I have been speaking?

I well remember, some years ago, when a boat was upturned in the rapids of Niagara, and one of its occupants, swept down the stream, caught desperate hold of a rock just above the falls. There he clung for long, long weary hours. Crowds gathered. Neighboring cities were telegraphed for implements of rescue. The interest and excitement grew intense. All manner of devices were suggested for reaching the imperiled man. One thing after another was tried and failed. Oh, what busy hands, swift feet, active minds, anxious hearts there were, all for the rescue of that one man. But help failed to reach him. He grew weaker and weaker, and at last let go the only thing that kept him from destruction.

There are persons whom we know to-day to be in far worse peril than that. We see them. They are before our eyes. We meet them in our homes, in our Sunday-school classes, in our social circles, here in this house of God. Some of them are personally very dear to us. It is the eternal death of the soul, they are in peril of. If they are not, then burn your Bibles and shut up the churches. I ask again, will you tell me what a gospel of salvation means, and why a gospel of salvation should be preached, that saves from nothing? If they are in peril, then the peril is imminent and deadly, be-

cause the death is the death of the soul. Some of
them are far down the rapids. Some possibly have
reached the last rock to which they can cling.
Oh, how often that rock is the memory of a godly
mother's prayers. Souls will sometimes cling there,
and hold to that memory as if they knew that to
be swept away from that would be to be carried
beyond the reach of mercy. And I do not wonder.
If I were an impenitent child of godly parents, and
should die so, I would rather go into eternity facing
a legion of devils than my mother's prayers. But
the hold of even a mother's prayers is weakening.
Every day the steady downward current of evil
is telling on the strength with which that memory is held. Christians, you must to the rescue, or
you will be too late.

Go, I beseech you, and amidst the gloom and
desolation and awful shadows that this subject casts
before, hold up Christ's blood-stained cross, the
beacon of hope, the herald of salvation, the promise
of deliverance, the joy of the disconsolate, the light
of life, the rock of ages, the savior of sinners, the
gift of God.

Here, I lift it again to-day: "Behold and believe," says the voice of the Lord. Standing in the
Lord's stead, I repeat the blessed words: "Behold
and believe!"

VIII.

CHRISTIANITY AND ENDLESS LIFE.

No human capacity ever yet saw the whole of a thing; but we may see more and more of it the longer we look.

—RUSKIN.

The gift of God is eternal life through Jesus Christ.

—THE APOSTLE PAUL.

On earth, in heaven, everywhere throughout the universe, this is eternal life—the only eternal life known to Christianity—union or reunion of the created mind with God.

—JOHN YOUNG.

CHRISTIANITY AND ENDLESS LIFE.

If man is to die at last like a dog, why should he live like an angel? If death ends all, then it would be difficult to prove that the " Let us eat and drink for to-morrow we die " philosophy is not the true one. On a question as to enjoyment or employment, laughter or labor, toying or toiling, the merry-makers would be likely to have the best of it. But if there is a life after death the conditions of which are decided by the life this side of death, and decided in such way that the conditions are ever-lasting, and if one way of going through the world makes them conditions of sorrow, and another way of going through the world makes them conditions of joy, it ought to make a mighty difference in our view of "the loaves and fishes" theory of life. Baser and nobler being begin to take on an infinite meaning, as being is stamped with immortality, and men are made to feel the everlasting—to stand in the face of it, live in the light of it, gather motive from it.

This is what Christianity compels men to do, whenever it gets a candid hearing. Everywhere through its record it sounds out the thought of eternity. Christianity is meaningless if life is to be snuffed out at last like a candle. It asserts and assumes, in the repose of sublimest confidence, that there is to be perpetuated existence beyond the grave. As living and convincing proof that death does not end all, it offers the resurrection of its Christ from the dead. And this amazing fact is so set round and buttressed up with corroboration of its reality, that no suggested theory of fraud or fanaticism by which to account for it, has ever yet won any wide acceptance from intelligent unbelief.

But not only does Christianity confront men with this thought of eternity—it confirms their fears with reference to the conditions of that eternity, if they go on as they are and "die in their sins." Through all the centuries and in all climes the altars have smoked with sacrifices for sin, as men have sought thus to get rid of their haunting apprehensions of a world beyond this. Christianity speaks in solemn confirmation of these apprehensions; says there is reason for these fears; makes certain what was imagined and guessed, and more or less distinctly defined in human consciousness. But it does not leave men with this disclosure. It illuminates the track of doom—not in any joy of the revelation, but for warning and rescue.   While it would have men know where they are going, it would have them go where perpetuated being will be perpetuated and ever increasing delight.   So it presents an alternative.   It makes an offer.   It presses a tremendous motive.

While it tells men of everlasting death, it offers men everlasting life.   It takes this idea of indestructible being, and though it paints the shadows until they deepen into a very "blackness of darkness" along sin's eternal path, it tells men they need not walk there—for "*the gift of God is eternal life through Jesus Christ.*"

Now while we may not grasp in anything like its amplitude and glory this "eternal life," which is God's gift to every man however lost to manhood, and however sunk in sin, who comes to believe in the Son of God and to accept Him as his personal Savior, we can gather many definite things· from the gospel record concerning it, that may possibly be corrective of false notions, and that may be persuasives to its joyful acceptance.

1. This, first, that the eternal life which is God's gift is *not all in the future world.*

The impression is widely prevalent that the rewards of Christian discipleship are a matter of expec-

tation.   Eternal life is thought to have to do solely
with eternity.   The common conception of it is of
something vague and ethereal.   Far too exclusively
it is referred to, as if its realities were impossible
of realization to any extent whatever this side of
the grave.

But the truth is, eternal life begins on the instant of a personal, believing acceptance of Jesus
Christ.   To this effect is repeated apostolic testimony.   "This is the record, that God hath given
to us eternal life, and this life is in his Son.   He
that hath the Son hath life."   To "know him that
is true," and to be "in Him that is true, even in
his Son Jesus Christ—this is eternal life."   And
Jesus himself said, "He that heareth my word and
believeth ...... hath everlasting life, and shall not
come into condemnation; but is passed from death
unto life."   Hence the terms, "new creature,"
"born again" or "born from above," "life out of
death," "created anew."   When that change occurs
which answers to these terms, the eternal life begins.
And therefore the righteous enter upon their eternal life when they become righteous, i. e., when
they by faith appropriate the righteousness of
Christ and so become heirs of an incorruptible inheritance.   They do not enter into all the fulness
of that inheritance, but they do get foretastes and

antepasts of the exceeding and external weight of glory.

Exactly what this eternal life is, it may be somewhat difficult to define, but in general it may be said to be the presence of a new principle in the soul—a principle of holiness planted there of God the Spirit—a disposition averse to evil, and that allies the soul with God, and makes fellowship with Him a dear delight. The blessednesses of this life are peace of conscience, sense of pardon and reconciliation with God, joyful communion with Christ and more and more likeness to Him in every sweet grace, as the years go on and God does His transforming and beautifying work in the heart.

This is not largely outward, it does not strike the eye, it does not appeal to the sense; it may consist with failure in worldly plans, and poverty in earthly treasures and loss of earthly friends; but does not all our truest joy hang on what we *are* and how we are conditioned *within?* Because a man has success in trade, and large accumulation of wealth, and ability to command all appliances for ease and comfort and æsthetic and social gratification, is he happy? He may be; but it is not his riches, nor his success in trade, nor his brilliant social relations that make him so. If he do not carry

13

sources of joy within him, into the midst of his riches, he will get very little joy from these outside things. I have been in princely homes, where everything was commanded that wealth could buy, and I have found skeletons there that made those homes more like sepulchres, whose brilliant garnishing seemed the saddest of mockeries and whose appearance of joy seemed the hollowest of pretentious shams. And I have been in homes of poverty that were like outer courts of heaven, enriched with all the riches of God. True joy is joy within, joy of soul, in truth, in love, in the good and the beautiful. It is the joy which Jesus left as a legacy to his disciples. That joy must be in us, before our joy can be full. It comes to the children of God in some measure when they first believe. It increasingly comes to them, in deeper and more blessed measure as their life goes on, if they open their hearts to its inward flow. In witness whereof, mark the testimony of an Apostle willing to suffer "the loss of all things" that he may know more of Christ. Listen to another Apostle on the victorious heights of Christian confidence, "glorying in tribulations." Hear the intellectual Edwards, so grandly endowed with reason that he could never be deemed a mere emotional enthusiast, telling of the blessedness and joy that came to his soul in such a tide that he felt he could not live, if God did not stay it. Take the case of Payson almost torn asunder with the spasms of bodily anguish, yet in his inward spirit and under the communications of God to the soul, filled with serene, ineffable delight. Take humble Christians this world over, finding joy in service and sacrifice, and content-ment every where, and rest in trouble, and comfort in sorrow, and hope in disappointment, and *Christ in all!* And be sure from this and much else that might be named, that the blessedness and peace and joy of eternal life are not all in the future. I have dwelt at length on this point, because the earthly Christian life is so commonly regarded as the self-denying and joyless way of purchasing the heavenly life, where and where only it is thought the joys and rewards of Christian discipleship are realized and the blessedness of the life-eternal is first experienced.

2. The second thing I have to say of the eternal life is that *it is not the same and never will be the same to all the saved.* Heaven is no sea of bliss where the righteous are to float in equal and ever-lasting content. Future blessedness is no common, ethereal state, where ethereal beings shall sing ethereal psalms. Eternal life is not a dead level to all who enter upon it. The gift of God is given to

all who believe in Jesus, and the gift is eternal life. But there is nothing more infinitely varied than life, any life. It nowhere finds manifestation in exactly the same forms. Take animal life— what a vast difference—what an infinite diversity; oyster and Leviathan; crawling parasite and soar- ing eagle. Take mental life—what two minds have exactly the same condition, and capacities, and methods? No two trees are the counterpart each of the other. Nay, no two leaves are such. Life every- where is in vast and endless variety. So it is with life eternal, that gift of God, constituting in its length, and breadth, and height, and depth, the re- wards of the righteous. There is one glory of the sun, and another of the moon, and another of the stars; for one star differeth from another star in glory. The penitent dying thief is not going into heaven like the triumphant dying Paul. The man who is saved so as by fire, his work of wood, hay and stubble all burned, is not to have the same reward as the man with an abundant entrance into heaven, his work of gold and silver and precious stones abiding, bearing the test, and passing through the fire without being consumed. Remember the word of the Lord to the ten servants en- trusted with ten pounds. On the reckoning day, one came, saying, Lord, thy pound hath gained ten.   And the Lord said, Well, thou good servant, have thou authority over ten cities.   And another came, saying, Lord, thy pound hath gained five. And the Lord said, Be thou over five cities.   The reward was according to the service.   Not of debt, but of grace.   "Lay up for yourselves treasures in heaven," said the Master.   We can do it.   We are doing it, by what we are, and how we live, and love, and pray.   Eternal life is the portion of every one who believes—it is the gift of God through Jesus; but the forms of it, the manifestations of it, the capital of it, and the capacities and accumulations—the riches, and glories, and joys of it, will be as varied as the fidelities, and the struggles and the consecrations, and the services rendered in the temporal and earthly life.   The life-long criminal, hoary with iniquity, steeped to the full in sin and transgression, and yielding only the fag-ends of his godless life to God, if the surrender be in penitent and believing sincerity, will be accepted in the all-embracing love of the Father, and will be admitted to heaven.   The blood of Jesus is equal to that ransom.   But that poor recovered wreck will get no such investment and experience of glory and of joy, as he who after high service for God on earth mounts up to heaven on the wings of a triumphant faith, saying, " I have fought a good fight, I have finished my course, I have kept the faith." To make their heaven the same heaven, their life the same life, their reward the same reward, is against analogy, against reason, against the word of God. There will be points of resemblance, but points of wide contrast, too. There will be some things in common characterizing each. There will be other things most different, deepening and enriching one life far above the other.

Let us see from the light of Scripture what all who are heirs of eternal life will have in common.

Freedom from sin. That is one thing, and a grand thing in the life of the sons and daughters of God. Moral evil will be eliminated forever. There, there entereth nothing that defileth. The blood of Jesus cleanseth from all sin. No matter what the difference in condition here, that blood applied to human hearts will secure entire sinlessness there. The penitent and believing publicans and harlots entering the kingdom of heaven will be clean, every whit—as perfectly free from pollution as the white-robed angels who have never been defiled with the pitch of sin. The soul of the penitent malefactor, seamed and ridged and blackened through and through as it may have been with the smoke and fire and mad riot of passion and lust up to the very hour of his execution, will be as spotlessly pure as the soul of the little child lifted out of its mother's arms into the bosom of God. Nothing tainted with moral evil can enter heaven. The poison of sin will never be allowed there. There will be no evil done, and no thought of evil, and no desire that way.

We all know how it is now; how sin and selfishness mar our best service; how thoughts come trooping in upon us most unwelcome; how we are wronged by others in deed and word and thought; and how we are prone to wrong them. All this will be ended in the sanctified life of the redeemed in heaven; ended with all of them when they come to die and pass up to the skies. It enters into and is common to the rewards of all the righteous, *freedom from sin.*

Freedom from suffering and sorrow, follows from this as another condition common to all life in heaven. The inhabitant shall no more say, I am sick. There shall be no more pain. Tears will be wiped away forever. No bodily aches, no fevers, no exhaustions, no thrills of physical torture; and no mental trouble, no anguish of spirit, no pangs of conscience, no jealousies and bickerings and distrusts will be there. *Sin* is the prolific source of suffering here. But the sinless place will be painless and sorrowless. And this, too, will be

200 CHRISTIANITY AND ENDLESS LIFE.

common to all the saved. A Mary Magdalene will be just as free from suffering in mind and body as Mary, the mother of Jesus. The sinner saved in the eleventh hour, and so as by fire, will be just as exempt from every shade of sorrow and every form of pain as the sainted man of God who, through a half century has turned many unto righteousness, and preached the gospel around the world.

Freedom from death, too, will be another condition common to all the saved. This is involved in the very idea of life as given of God. That gift eternal makes death and every concomitant of death forever impossible. The resurrection and the life will have swallowed up death in victory. Body and spirit will be broken forever away from his fell dominion and power. There will be no growing weakness, no decrepitude, no decay and dissolution, no turning to the dust again, no graves opening along heaven's paths and crying, "Give, give." And there will be no death of soul, no spiritual death, no approaches to it or likeness of it, no blackness of darkness of death from the hidings of God's face and the frowns of his justice, but life, positive, uninterrupted, endless, cloudless. "My sheep hear my voice and they follow me. And I give unto them eternal life, and *they shall never perish.*

The gift of God is eternal life. Once saved, and the soul, any soul, every soul, is just as fully assured · of perpetual freedom from death, as is the Infinite author of life himself—Jehovah, God.

To this extent the teachings of Scripture make it plain, the eternal life will be shared alike by all the saved. The word of God makes these things common to all who believe in Jesus. Indeed, salvation in the gospel sense is impossible without them. A bare salvation implies them and necessitates them. They are the promised conditions of the future life common to all. And thus far heaven is one. My heaven and your heaven, if we truly believe in Jesus, and the believing harlot's heaven, and Paul's heaven, and Abraham's, and Isaac's, and Jacob's, and the heaven of the Son of God, will have alike these characteristics; it will be sinless, sorrowless, deathless.

But this is all negative, and life is positive; this is passive, and life is active; this is fixedness, and life is development. Blessed as it will be to be rid of sin, to be rid of sorrow, to be rid of death, it is only the blessedness of negation. The powers, capacities, endowments, gifts, graces, possibilities, attainments, accumulations on the positive side now come in for consideration. *And here the saved part company;* here the eternal life ceases to be

common, and becomes different; here the blessedness of the righteous gets degrees, and varying pro-
portions and differing altitudes, according as their
several pounds entrusted to them of God have
gained in the earthly stewardship, ten or five, or
two or one.

Take two ideas warranted by God's word, concerning this eternal life, the capacities that may be
developed, and the treasures that may be laid up in
its progress. First, the capacities that may be developed. All life has development for its law, and
spiritual life is not an exception. The Bible recog-
nizes differing capabilities in this life of God; speaks
of great faith and little faith; a cold love and a
burning, absorbing love; a knowledge that is weak,
seeing through a glass darkly, and a knowledge
face to face; an infancy in Jesus, and a maturing
manhood, a growth upward, unto the measure of the
stature of Christ's fulness into the same image, from
glory to glory, as if there were no limitation to the
soul's possibilities in its ascending march to the divine heights where God is beckoning it. Paul
passed up some of these heights before he died.
His faith was strong, his love ardent, his knowledge great, his comprehension of things spiritual,
vast. He grew as he labored. He won enlarging
capacity in his laborious toils. Other men have

done the same and women too. Saints of God in all ages since, have grown glorious in spiritual stature, have seen far into the deep things of God; have grasped mysteries of faith and love, have fathomed depths and scaled heights, have developed capabilities and powers, as they have toiled and prayed, and loved and wrestled, and studied and pondered, and opened their hearts and minds to the revealing Spirit, and been led of Him into all truth. Think of the dying Payson, though racked with pain, yet swimming in a sea of glory. Think of the dying Scott, going down into the valley of death, saying, "This is heaven begun. I have done with darkness forever, forever." Think of the men that have been distinguished for their walk with God—the godly McCheyne and Edwards, and Chalmers and Baxter, and Alexander, and Barnes and Skinner. These have commenced their heavenly life, enriched and enlarged far beyond the measure of millions of others who have gone into heaven just as free from sin and sorrow and death.

Take now the other idea, the treasures that may be laid up. What they are, I do not attempt definitely and positively to say. But *that they are laid up* by those who are faithful, we have the Master's own word for. They are being put away there of

204 CHRISTIANITY AND ENDLESS LIFE.

the infinite God, to be brought out and given to the faithful toilers, when they shall be called from the field of labor. The Psalmist burst forth with this grand thought as he sang, "O how great is thy goodness which thou hast laid up for them that fear thee, which thou hast wrought out for them that trust in Thee before the sons of men." The spiritual athletes, the self-denying toilers, the walkers with God, those that fellowship most lovingly and yearningly and intimately with Jesus, those counting all things but loss for Him, and proving it by the way they live and love and labor, have the largest investments and the greatest gains. It must be so. We have divine intimations of it, precious scriptural hints and suggestions answering to, and fortifying, this natural expectation of our hearts.

We are not all going to enter upon the same life. In some respects it will be the same. In others it will be widely in contrast and different, just as our fidelities in service and sacrifice here have differed. Mere freedom from sin will not lift the soul to the highest altitudes of spiritual efficiency and power and perception. Mere freedom from suffering will not lift a soul into that perfected and exalted bliss of being which some surely have entered as they have entered heaven. Mere freedom from death will not transform into the highest and divinest life.

But, it is objected, if one is entirely happy in heaven, without sin and without sorrow, happy according to one's measure, to the full, what brooks it that others with larger capital and spiritual capabilities and acquisitions, have larger degree of happiness according to their measure? This. A snail is happy according to its measure. So is a free and soaring lark. Is there no preference between the two? A child is happy, with a circumference of joy, struck by the shortest radius—happy according to its measure. So is a man, with his developed and richly stored mind and heart, as pure as the child, yet unfolded and enlarged, so as to strike the circumference of a thousand fold greater and deeper joy than the child. Is there no preference between the two? Is it all one whether I listen contentedly and delightedly, with an uncultivated ear, to the rudest melody, satisfied with it because I can appreciate that and no more—or whether I listen, thrilled and entranced, with a cultivated ear, to the most delicious harmonies, because my soul is educated and attuned to the higher musical excellence? The case is too clear for question. To say for a soul to be happy according to its measure is enough—is to say it is just as well to be one remove from a laughing idiot, as to be a high intelligence amidst the presence and throne-angels of God. It is better, vastly better, and it will be better everlastingly, to have an abundant entrance and a large reward in heaven, than to be saved so as by fire, with only negations to start with in the life to come.

3. The eternal life as it is comprehended and experienced *will be increasingly blessed and glorious forever and ever.* It is life's law to develop. And eternal life is eternal development. We cannot take that in. We do not know what that means. We do not know what we shall be. But it means, among other things that are inconceivable, some things that we may comprehend. It means a memory that shall lose nothing, a mind that shall pervert nothing, a heart that shall repel nothing, but love on, and reason on, and store on, through illimitable ages, having the freedom of God's universe, and possibilities of glory and wisdom and affection and power exceeding abundantly above all we can tell or think. Everything that God has will be spread out and laid open to the children of God. The riches of God's creative wisdom and love, the riches of His grace, the riches of His glory, the kingdoms of creation, redemption and reward piled one above another, in every direction an absolutely inconceivable infinitude—what heart can conceive, what mind measure these things? We

are confounded by the very attempt, and can only cry with the enraptured, yet baffled apostle, O the depths, the infinite depths of the riches of the wisdom and knowledge and love of God! How unsearchable are they! How past finding out!

And as these riches unfold, the increasing knowledge will bring increasing joy. The joys of the righteous from the very constitution of their life, must be positively and infinitely progressive. This is of God and it is all we can say about it. It is a power and a mystery of bliss beyond all mortal conceiving. It is God's own mystery, God's own glory, God's own gift, God's sole almighty power, revealing himself in undiminished freshness and novelty to the righteous though ages on ages, giving to them as his gift of eternal life *a capacity of bliss forever enlarging and a reality of bliss forever accumulating.*

This is life—eternal life, purchased for and brought to and given every believer in Christ Jesus. It is partially realized at the very beginning of the Christian life; it is of varying beauty and blessedness and glory according to the service rendered and spiritual development secured, and the accumulations made; and it is capable of boundless increase, for it is everlasting. God be praised that we have the possibility of such an infinitely perfect and glorious salvation. God be praised that Jesus is able to raise us out of such an abyss of ruin as Christianity tells us we are rushing into, to such a height of joy and glory as Christianity promises to every one that believeth.

The ruin is before you, child of sin, but you need not share it. Hell is a reality, sinner against God, but you need not enter it. It would be an utterly false benevolence in me to shrink from making known to you your guilt and danger. It would be a lying sympathy and a most reprehensible and contemptible dread of giving offence, if I should neglect to say, what the Lord Jesus with profound emphasis and solemn earnestness has said, He that believeth not the Son shall not see life, but the wrath of God abideth on him. But true and awful as it is, that the wages of sin is death, and that if you continue in the service of sin you will be paid sin's dreadful wages—it is also as true that *the gift of God is eternal life through Jesus Christ.* O take the gift, if it be not already yours by faith, take this free and boundless gift of life— believe in Jesus and become an heir of God and a joint heir with Christ to the inheritance " that is incorruptible and undefiled and that fadeth not away."

IX.

CHRISTIANITY AND PLEASURE.

He buys honey too dear who licks it from thorns.
—OLD PROVERB.

This same truth is a naked and open daylight, that does not show the masks and mummeries and triumphs of the world half so stately and daintily as candle lights.
—LORD BACON·

Gladness is sown for the upright in heart.
—THE PSALMIST.

Fly the pleasure which bites to-morrow.—PROVERB.

CHRISTIANITY AND PLEASURE.

Of all the goodly fellowship of the Prophets, the Old Testament saint who most completely voices the experience of Christian hearts, is he who went *singing* through the world. Praises and thanksgivings and aspirations and adorations still flow in great tides of joy through his speech. "The Psalms" get thumbed as no other scriptures do, save where David's Lord himself appears.

Yet David knew something of sorrow. There were days of his full of mourning and bitterness, when his songs were changed into sighings. But his very griefs sent him sounding the depths of more blessed experiences, so that his sighs changed back again into songs, and joys flashed from the very swing of his sorrows. Praise was most often upon his lips, and he thanked God with a healthy, robust heartiness that put it past all doubt that it was joyful tribute he brought. Joy must have beamed in the eye and glowed in the face, even as it flowed out in the speech and the song, of this sweet singer of Israel.

It has come down the centuries. It is as much a fruit of Christian trust to-day as when David swept his glad harp. " I will be glad and rejoice in thee" sang the Psalmist. "Bless the Lord, O my soul, and forget not all his benefits." "Sing unto the Lord, O ye saints of His, and give thanks." "Let the righteous be glad: let them rejoice before the Lord; yea, let them rejoice exceedingly." "Shout for joy all ye that are upright in heart." And the Apostle, ages after, takes up the strain, and says: "Rejoice in the Lord always, and again I say rejoice." The kingdom of God is not gloom and unrest, but "joy and peace." And the fruit of the Spirit is "peace and joy." Peace like a river—joy unspeakable.

But this is not the common estimation. This is not the world's way of looking at it. Religion gets painted with a sad countenance. Christianity is prevalently regarded as opposed to pleasure; its flowers a night-shade; its psalms a *miserere*; its joys after death, not this side of it. "God is thought a hard creditor; man a poor debtor; religion the sum he is to pay." Hence, to be pious is esteemed a melancholy sort of a thing, an abandonment of dear delights, and an entrance upon a kind of House of Correction work. Many devotees of the world look at it, not as a thing good in itself, but as an unnatural self-denial, to be avoided if one dared— a burden and a weariness in this life, to help one get "saved" in the next. The often ackowleged, and more often unacknowledged though really present and controlling reason for not entering upon Christian discipleship is the reluctance to give up worldly joy.

The idea is cherished that joy must be turned out of doors before religion can come in; that the pious must put on moral gyves and hand-cuffs and go restrained, burdened, joyless through the world. The young, at least, are not ready for that. They mean to rejoice in their youth and opening manhood and womanhood, and to freely quaff the wine of the world's delights, and by and by, when the freshness of life is gone, and their hearts have cheered them with earthly things until the delicious zest and sweetness of their enjoyment are gone, they purpose to be religious and join the Church, and go soberly and devoutly and self-denyingly the rest of the earthly way, so as to meet the requisite gospel conditions and obtain a share of eternal happiness.

Now this view of religion, prevailing so largely in the gay circles of worldly life, certainly does not square with the scriptural representations. Christian experience is there set forth as a thing of bounding delights. "Rejoice in the Lord always." "Serve Him with gladness." "Shout aloud for joy." "Enter His gates with thanksgiving." "Be glad and rejoice ye righteous." "Gladness is sown for the upright in heart." The Gospel is called "good tidings of great joy." Of a city where it greatly spread, it is said, "There was great joy in that city." Christians are spoken of as rejoicing in Christ with joy unspeakable and full of glory, and as rejoicing in God's word, as one that findeth great spoil. The kingdom of heaven is likened unto treasure hid in a field; the which, when a man hath found, for joy thereof, he buyeth, selling all that he hath that he may make the joy-giving treasure his own. There is nothing of the sombre and the austere about all this. A prevailingly sad countenance is impossible in such moods of the spirit.

How happens it then that Christianity is so frequently thought to be opposed to pleasure?

1. It arises from *false notions of what Christianity really is and requires*. A nun, a monk, a hermit, a rigid recluse, is not a representative of the Christian religion. Yet these, who have become infidel to society, turning their backs upon what God has ordained in the social state, have

been set up by the Church as models, and com-
mended as pre-eminent examples of devotion.
Read the record of such a life as that of St. Hugh,
Archbishop of Lyons. It was his "constant
prayer that God would extinguish in his heart all
attachment to creatures." "His love of heavenly
things made all temporal affairs seem burdensome
and tedious." "Women he would never look in
the face, so that he knew not the features of his
own mother." How utterly at war all this with
the dearest instincts of our hearts, and how utter
the misconception of the religion of Him who put
holy seal upon marriage by his gracious presence
and miraculous blessing, who loved Martha and
Mary and Lazarus in that dear home in Bethany,
and one of whose dying acts was a tender provision
for his own mother. Yet it is just such morbid exhibitions of devotion that have been extolled by
the Church of Rome. Piety has been symbolized
by monkish seclusion, content with parched peas
and a water-cress. Ecclesiastical fanaticism has
fettered the senses, put them in duress, tortured
them to silence, made a blank solitude, and called
it peace. The fulness and frequency of fastings,
the abundance of mortifications, and the number
of repeated prayers, have been the exalted tests of
religious faithfulness. And those wearing dark,

sad, woe-stained faces, have been honored with saint-hood, and their pictures hung round the walls of convents and cathedrals. As if black were the color of heaven! As if a resemblance to midnight were a proof of grace! The God who says the fast he has chosen is not to spread sackcloth and ashes, but to loose the bands of wickedness, to undo the heavy burdens, to break every yoke, to deal bread to the hungry and covering to the naked, the God who gave us flowers and carolling birds, and who so often wreathes and girdles the green earth with smiles, never sent his servants into the world to live such a lie as that.

The burden of the Gospel message is glad tidings of great joy to all people. Change that, and put the lie upon it by making a mock at joy and renouncing it—above all by renouncing it in the name of God, and the world will swing inevitably to the opposite extreme of reckless dissipation.

2. Another reason for the prevalent impression that Christianity is opposed to pleasure is this: the *austere and unsmiling mien of so many Christians*, in connection with their religious life. They wear sad countenances. They seem slaves at reluctant toil, instead of glad freemen in Christ Jesus. They go moaning and mourning where

they ought to go singing songs of gladness. They take on looks that betoken anything but a residence in the temple where joy dwelleth.

Now a part of this seeming sadness may be justified and proved consistent with Christianity's claim to be a service of joy.

The deepest joy does not express itself in laughter, but in tears. The mother, getting back her loved child again, rescued from imminent and deadly peril—as she clasps it in her arms, *saved*, does she laugh? or weep? The song or the story that steals down into our hearts and opens the fountains where tears have their home— is not that the song or the story occasioning an inner delight, sweeter and deeper and richer far than that we express by rapturous applause? Who does not know that when we are fullest of joy, we are full to weeping? and that then there is a very luxury in tears? That then tears are joy's natural utterance? So it is, often, with God's people. Their dearest resorts are Valleys of Baca. Their choicest hours are when the fountains overflow. Their heavenliest experiences are tearful, for the very depths of joy they go sounding. They weep at their feasts of love, and they cannot help it, but a bow of promise and of love is set in every teardrop, for the glory of the sun of righteousness shining through.

Then again there are times when earnest, godly men are made acquainted with such ghastly forms of wickedness, and get so impressed with the sin and woe of the world, "the sad sight of private suffering, and the sadder sight of conscious and triumphant wickedness born with an arithmetic instead of a conscience, trampling the needy down to dust and treating the Almighty with sneer and scoff," that they cannot help wearing an earnest, sad, exceeding sorrowful face. But Christianity is not what puts such look on them. They see the dominance in the world's heart, of that hell of evil which is opposed to Christianity: and *that* makes them take on at times so sad an earnestness. It is only Christianity with its blessed hopes and promises that can ever wash that sadness out of their faces. But with all due allowance for this, let it be confessed, there is much of sombre-hued piety for which there is no excuse; and which misrepresents religion, instead of illustrating and adorning it. You will see Christians held to the Lord's service by slavish fear. Their *consciences* have compelled them to take sides, not their hearts. They get no joy from their religion. It is no wonder, therefore, that no joy beams in their faces, when they are discharging religious duties. It is not in the nature of a thing that is irksome to give a sparkle to the eye, and buoyancy to step, and lightness to the spirit. But mark such Christians, when the restraints of Christian service are off and the forms of godliness are put away. See the flush of the face and the flash of the eye, and the eager, bounding joy of the spirit, as religion is forgotten in the whirl of pleasure. The world notes such contrasts, and says, "Christianity is hostile to enjoyment and repressive of joy; for these people, as soon as they get away from religious duties, are glad enough." But what an unjust and shameful inference! It is a want of Christianity and not Christianity itself, that makes so many Christians wear a weary, sad, unsmiling look when at their worship and service for God. They make hard work of their piety, because their piety is not allowed to make much work with them. They do not like it. Their whole hearts are not in it. They browse along the borders of the goodly land, instead of entering into the rich pastures thereof. They live at a cold distance from Christ, instead of getting near enough to taste the best and rarest sweets of Christian discipleship. It is out of all reason to expect that from such following, joy shall come. Christianity is not at fault. It is the fearful absence of it, that dresses in such doleful, dismal, cheerless garb the piety of some professors. Will you get heat from an iceberg? or the song of the soaring lark from a toad? or the touch of softness from solid granite? Well, neither can you get the glow and gladness of joyous, bounding Christian life from a dead form. If the dead form hang out its appropriate signals, do not say these funeral weeds are the sign and fruit of religious life. If these miserable formalists look sad and go sighing and whining to their pious toil do not charge it upon Christianity.

3. A third occasion for the impression that Christianity is opposed to pleasure *is the character of its doctrines.* It is constantly telling of sin and its condemnation. Its preachers, it is said, are never done with exposing human depravity and warning against retribution. It must be a dark-visaged and gloomy thing that comes thrusting itself into the world with such heralding. But if the revelation be the truth, is it not best for man to know it? And if along with the disclosure of the disease there is offered an all-sufficient remedy, is Christianity to be thought gloomy and joyless?

You are afflicted with a painful˜ and offensive tumor. A physician tells you it is deadly, and lances and probes ·it, for your healing. It is not a very pleasant thing to do—neither pleasant to him nor you. But what kind of reason is there in saying the physician is opposed to pleasure because he does it.

You are carelessly sporting in a small boat some distance above Niagara's rapids, whiling away the precious moments, heedless of the increasing swiftness of the current, and of the increasing clearness of the roar of the cataract, and of your near approach to what will be ere long inevitable destruction. Or you are sleeping, dreaming dreams, reveling in a region of rare delight, all unconscious of the flames that are licking their way up the walls of your dwelling, and steadily, stealthily approaching your couch of slumber. It might be a rude startling from your pleasant pastime, or a rude waking from your dreamy sleep; but he who should rouse you to a sense of your peril, or provide a sure escape—you would scarcely speak of him as opposed to pleasure.

Is Christianity long-visaged and gloomy, a foe to joy, because it tells you of your moral wound and probes it for healing, providing and prescribing unfailing remedy? Is Christianity sad-countenanced and an enemy of pleasure, because it startles you from your death-sleep, and warns you of impending danger and bids you flee while yet there is possibility and hope of escape? Christianity does come, telling of sin and condemnation—

and these are not pleasant things to hear. But if they are true, it certainly is best to know them. If you are smitten with a moral malady that has struck through and through every fibre of your soul, and Jesus Christ is a good physician, bringing the only balm in this wide world efficacious for your healing—if you are a sinner before God, guilty and condemned, exposed to merited retribution, and Jesus Christ is a Savior come into the world to suffer in your stead, and by his blood to redeem you from sin and to wash you clean of its pollution, then you are certainly guilty of the folly of calling evil good, and good evil, if you denounce Christianity as dismal and gloomy because it tells you all this. Christianity does not *make* your sin and condemnation. There they are, the sad, dark, woeful realities of life. Your being indifferent to them, careless about them, unconscious of them, does not do away with them. The whirl of gay and alluring worldliness does not put them farther off, any more than the dream of the sleeper stops the advancing flames—or than the riotous indulgence of one smitten with deadly disease, stops the approach of it to the vitals. By and by, sin and condemnation will make their reality felt, and there will be no remedy. *Now*, Christianity comes with its glad tidings of great joy, saying, there is balm in Gilead and a good Physician there. Surely, for a human soul diseased, that is anything but a cheerless and joyless thing to know.

4. But a fourth reason, why Christianity is thought to be opposed to pleasure is *its demanded self-denial.*

The gospel does summon men to a kind of crucifixion—and crucifixion hurts. We sacrifice self, and cross natural desire, and compel a passion to go ungratified at a cost. But there is no disguising the matter. Christianity demands just this. It says, Take up thy cross. Self-sacrifice is its inner and essential law. And the world says, "No. Away with this gloomy, self-afflicting asceticism. God has not given us tastes and aptitudes and delicious capabilities of enjoyment, only to have them denied and crucified. Christianity is opposed to pleasure. We will have none of it."

But the denial called for by Christianity, is not of all natural tastes. Jesus was at weddings and feasts and social entertainments. He found joy in society. But he found his highest joy in service and sacrifice for others. He delighted to do God's will. It was his meat and drink. He lost himself, forgot himself, in those whom he came to seek and save. And this is the denial that he demands of his followers: denial of self; the crucifixion of selfishness; the going out of self into Him, and the living in Him and for Him; and so finding the motive power of all true life—not one's own interests, passions, desires, but the interest and advance of others.

Now what is this, but stepping up into a higher life—a blesseder and more joy-giving life, than that which is found on the lower level of selfishness? It is at a cost indeed, that the step is taken. It hurts thus to crucify—it is a cross we take up—nay, to which we may be nailed; but out of the crucifixion comes an exquisite pleasure, swallowing up the pain, and making the cross a means of uplifting to a greater joy. This is the Lord's way: "Take my *yoke* upon you, and ye shall find rest." Who does not know that life is dearest and richest when merged in that of another? What are wearying vigils and wearing care to a mother, watching over her child? They cost something. But there is no joy to her, like the joy of that martyrdom. She lives in and for her offspring, and the very sacrifices her love makes, are the occasions of that gladness that most thrills and satisfies her soul. Men forget this—the world forgets it—when Christianity is heard saying, Deny thyself. They think of the pain only. They forget the joy that swallows it up. They think of the yoke only. They forget "the rest" that comes from taking the yoke. They think only of the loss of the lower, selfish life. They forget the gain of the higher, unselfish life—the blissful and blessed life of God, into the outskirts of which every man enters the moment he denies self, takes up his cross and follows Jesus, and into the fulness of which he one day enters when he comes wholly to lose himself and wholly to hide his life with Christ in God.

And now, having sought to clear Christianity of the misrepresentations of some, and the misconceptions of others, let me briefly indicate its exact posture, with reference to pleasures that are not spiritual.

In the first place, it *frowns on the harmful*. Any indulgence that tends to abuse of soul, mind, or body, Christianity forbids. And in this, certainly, Christianity is not alone. The actual commandments of God written on every fibre of human flesh, are just as clear and authoritative as those written on Sinai's tables of stone, or those found in the four gospels. If the natural gratification of the body is the thing desired, (and that is a legitimate thing to desire) it must not be against the body's law. That law condemns, equally with Christianity, the base imbruting of the body to carnal passions and lusts of the flesh. The penalty in either case, is

15

ultimate loss of capacity for pleasure, ending in corruption, rottenness, death. Everybody knows the joy of the senses. God has made them to be inlets and ministries of delight. But there are higher faculties of mind, bringing correspondingly higher joys. And still above these are the affectional powers. And higher yet, the religious. And over against them, according to their gratification, is delight rising above delight. Pleasures, therefore, that dwarf and blast these higher powers, in pandering to the sensual, are of course opposed by Christianity. Where man seems only an appendage to the table, as with the glutton; where the Devil rings a dollar in his ear, and he dreams of money every day, as with the miser; where right is discrowned and trampled on, as with the tyrant clutching at power; where the pith and sinew and glow and spring of life are being wasted away and utterly worn out in the whirl of reckless dissipation, as with many an amusement-seeker and killer of time,—there, and in all such places, Christianity writes peremptory prohibitions. Anything that does harm to any part of our nature, belittling the mind, soiling the spirit, impairing the vitality, undermining the health, anything that consciously lowers us, that puts us in contact with evil, that gives countenance to iniquity, that wrongs another, that works our own hurt, whatever the thrills and passions of ecstasy accompanying it—is condemned. And to this full extent, be it cheerfully admitted, Christianity frowns on pleasure.

Christianity *corrects the abuse of innocent sources of joy.* True religion is normal life—not of the religious powers, so called, alone, but of the whole man. It tends to keep every sense and every faculty in its place, subordinating the lower to the higher, but giving all their legitimate indulgence and gratification. The natural tendency is to excess. Christianity comes in to balance and poise us—not to give us the partial and transient joy of any one sense or faculty, but the complete and permanent joy of the whole man; the total and rounded delight of every part of our nature. It does not interfere with any natural and innocent delight—nor forbid the seeking such delight from any natural and innocent source. It is only regulative in these realms. It says, "Be diligent in business," but furnishes some golden rules for the prosecution of it, and counsels fervency of spirit as a companion, making even the common toil of life a kind of joy-giving sacrament. It does not forbid riches, and honor, and human applause, but warns against the love of them. Let men get joy from these if they will. But Christianity says, See to it that integrity of spirit is preserved, that the riches do not own you instead of you the riches, that self is subordinated in the earning and the use of these sources of delight, so that you shall be the manlier and mankind the richer, by reason of the acquired joy. Christianity moreover, does not forbid recreations. It only demands that they be without sin, not evil in their nature or their tendency, in themselves or their consequence, and without excess in their indulgence. It makes no sweeping and indiscriminate raid on recreative enjoyment, designed to charm us away from burdening care, and to round out the lighter and magnetic side of us. It is only jealous of the higher nature's purity and prerogatives, and careful to keep that balance in which alone the deepest and truest joy is conditioned. It has no frowns for the delights of music, but condemns, only when its strains are mingled with scenes and associations that soil the spirit by suggested uncleanness. It has no frowns for light and graceful exercise, but certainly is opposed to that abuse and perversion of it, where it must be taken by posturing one's self more or less in an other's arms.

There is nothing in Christianity opposed to the innocent laugh and joy of life; there is nothing inconsistent with those diverting pastimes of unob-

jectionable tendency and surroundings, which relieve the mind from its tension of toil, or stir the
blood with their bounding activities, or give the
rest and the recuperation which hard work has made
necessary, or pull delights up from the heart's
depths that break out on the air in ripples of laughter.   I can pray all the better, for forgetting my
praying in my playing.   Let that playing be innocent, let the pleasure I seek, and into which I may
go as heartily as I go into the grandest of Chris-
tion toil, be freed from evil influence, and my
very praying shall sanctify and sweeten it.   This
is the relation of Christianity to pleasure.   It does
enhance the joy of what it allows.   It sends us into
our amusements with a good conscience; with a
zest, a relish, not abused and dulled as to its edge
by excess of indulgence and ruinous dissipation;
with sensibilities needing no extra, artificial stimu-
lants to whip them into a condition where they
shall yield their wonted measure of delight.   It
says to every man accepting and adopting it,
whatsoever thy hands find to do, whether work or
play, do it with thy might.   Anything that it is
worth while to do, it is worth while to do with the
whole head and heart.   And Christianity is pleas-
ant-faced, not sombre-hued—a joyful, not a joyless
thing.   God has put mirthfulness in the human

soul. To laugh is to do one of those things that belong only to human nature—to man. How we all love to win the dear, winsome, dimpled proofs of gladness from the baby. Is there anything in Christianity that says, Stamp this out, repress it; let mirth and gladness and joyous delights go? God forbid. Keep aloof only from pleasures inimical to mind, body or soul. Taste no harmful joys. But use all else this winning, alluring, beautiful world has, guarding only against perversion and excess. Christianity allows and approves this. It condemns many things beyond a question, and some that can stir with a very thrill and passion of joy. There are exqusite ecstacies of delight, concerning which, Christianity says, " No! judge at your peril." But it says it, solely because the peril is there. These forbidden pleasures have a sting in them whose poison at the last will take away the capability and so the possibility of any joy.

Christianity endorses pleasures that are pure, wholesome, healthful, invigorating; and helps us get the more gladness out of them because we carry Christianity with us into them. And then it has joys of its own that the worldling can never know. Ah, I wish I could tell you all the feelings of my heart about this, my dear, Christless friend. But it is something that can never be fully told. O, the blessednesses of the man that walketh not in the counsel of the ungodly. But if the millions of hearts are to be believed that have testified, there are secrets of inner and satisfying and ravishing delights in connection with the Christian religion, so blissful and blessed, that they transform weakness into strength and sorrow into joy, and defeat into victory, and loss into gain, and trial into triumph, and death into life, even this side of Heaven! Has the most favored of all the devotees of pleasure ever gotten anything like that from the world? But that is not all. God is merely tuning the soul, as an instrument, in this life. And these joys of the Christians, are only the notes and chords that are sounded out in the preparation—preludes to the perfect harmony that shall flood the soul—forerunners of the perfected and rapturous joy that shall bless the soul, in that exceeding and eternal weight of glory.

I commend Christianity to you, not as opposed to pleasure—but as a source of pleasure. I ask you to read and receive this blessed gospel, in the spirit of its divine founder, not in the light of the cowl and the cloister. Joys long to be yours, better far than you have ever tasted. They come to your hearts, like birds, seeking inlet. They may sit and sing awhile, waiting for entrance. But they will

not always stay. If you let them fly away, they
may never come again. Never then shall be
known by you the peace that passeth understanding and the joy unspeakable and full of glory. O,
be sure.

> There are briers besetting every path,
>   That call for patient care,
> There is a cross in every lot,
>   And an earnest need for prayer;
> But the lowly heart that trusts in God
>   Is happy everywhere.

X.

CHRISTIANITY AND BUSINESS.

.

Prayer and provender hinder no man's journey.
                                        —Old Proverb.

A servant with this clause
    Makes drudgery divine.
Who sweeps a room as for thy laws
    Makes that and the action fine.
                                        —George Herbert.

Whatsoever ye do in word or deed, do all in the name of the Lord Jesus.—The Apostle Paul.

The devil tempts all; but the idle man tempts the devil.
                                        —Italian Proverb.

CHRISTIANITY AND BUSINESS.

Somewhere I have seen mention of a satirical poem in which the devil is represented as fishing for men, and fitting his baits to the taste and business of his prey; but the idler, he said, gave him no trouble, as he bit the naked hook. The ruin of many a soul has certainly dated from some vacant hour. They that do nothing are in the ready way to do worse than nothing. Employment is the necessity of human nature. It is contributive to physical vigor, to mental development, to cheerfulness of spirit, to moral safety. The body must have occupation to have and keep robustness. The mind must have something to do to attain to any degree of efficiency. The soil of the heart left fallow, will soon produce weeds. Employment is so certainly provocative of cheerfulness, that men have been known to come home in high spirits from some quite melancholy business because they had had the management of it. Activity is essential to vigorous life everywhere. And industry is a source of positive joy. " King Clog does not like King Jog," but King Jog gets by far the largest following; for there is a demand for something to do laid of God in the very constitution of our physical and mental and moral nature.

But here comes Christianity condemning the god of this world, and the wisdom of it, and the children of it, warning against the cares of this world and the deceitfulness of riches, as the thorns that will choke the good seed of the kingdom. Are we then to have no wordly cares? Is wealth to be avoided? Is secular activity hostile to piety? Must we fly business, and society and home, and seek the cloister in order to be most truly Christians? Oh no. The remedy for worldly pollution is not monastic asceticism. Body, mind, soul, alike demand activity. Give them work to do, therefore, and pleasure to enjoy, in God's own fair though sin-smitten world. But in all worldly employment let its true relation to religion be understood and kept. What is this relation?

It is not one of antagonism. The demand for physical and mental activity is so set in the very constitution of our nature, and its gratification is so essential to the perfecting and ennobling of our life in its natural relations, that it would place God's redemptive work in contradiction with His creative work, to set Christianity in opposition to the ordinary pursuits and callings of men. These pursuits are essential. What we call secular toil is a necessity. Men cannot live without labor. God has set the solitary in families, establishing society with all its intricate and diverse relationships; and He has endowed man with gifts and powers of action, and acquisition, and mutual help, and implanted the impulse to put these to their appropriate activity. God has no gospel that antagonizes all this. And He could be the author of no Christianity, whose highest development and life could not be attained in the midst of these secular activities. Eternal life is not to be had by renouncing the stirring business of temporal life. One need not neglect his farm or his merchandise, his office or his shop, to take care of his soul. There is no hostility between grace and trade. Godliness is profitable unto all things. We are incited to toil by a natural impulse. We are commanded to it by an outward necessity. Christianity is not to be charged with introducing an opposing necessity, as if business and religion were antagonistic. Being alike essential, they cannot be inimical. Yet there are multitudes who think work and worship operate to each others harm; that the one must be somewhat neglected, if the other is well attended to. I have heard men plead pressure of business again and again, as a reason for their want of interest in things spiritual, as if there were something essentially hostile to vital godliness, and inimical to piety in the work of the world. This is making God the author of a contradiction, for He has put man under the necessity of work, and under the necessity of worship. The doing of either cannot therefore be injurious to the other. Christianity does not condemn traffic, commerce, material activities of any kind. Its highest development is possible with the busiest life. To be a first-rate business man does not involve being a fourth-rate Christian. To enrich one's self at trade, it is not necessary to starve one's self at religion. The man that pleads his vast business as a reason for his little piety, libels the God who made him, and the Christianity that came from God. There have been men, the sails of whose commerce have whitened nearly all seas, and yet whose Christ-like lives and deeds of godliness, have reached even beyond their commerce. There have been men, they are living to-day, grandly successful in trade, wise in investments, occupied daily with widely extended financial and commercial interests, among the very best business men in the country, yet great layers up of treasures in heaven, and rich with the riches of God. Everywhere the world takes knowledge of them that they have been with

Jesus. Surely to be religious is not to be a ne'er-do-well in things temporal. Piety is not opposed to trade. There is no antagonism between Christianity and business.

2. But secondly, *the relation is not one of separation.* Christianity is not to be kept as a thing apart from business, away from it, unmixed with it, unaffected by business, and uninfluencing business. Very many, however, seem to think this is the true adjustment of the matter. They say there is no antagonism. No, their religion and business never interfere, the one with the other. They have a perfect understanding. We keep them both. We believe in them both. But business is business. Religion is religion. We have a place and a time for each. They are not opposed to each other. Of course not. They are simply kept apart; made to know their own place; put, as the farmer puts his apples and potatoes, in separate bins. The week is the bin for business, and Sunday is the bin for religion. Business has the mart, the shop, the office, and the counting room. Religion has the sanctuary. Over the doors where they drive bargains and prosecute gains, and make investments, and counsel clients, is written, "No admittance except on business." And all men understand that Christianity has no business with business. Over the

door of the sanctuary is written, "Devoted to Religion;" and all men understand that business has no business with that.

Hence come demands upon the pulpit to keep clear of what has been called secular preaching, or political preaching, i. e. preaching that deals with the actual sins of politics, of trade, of covetousness; preaching that goes fearlessly down into the every-day work of the week, and that makes religion a thing of common life, giving principles by which men are to cast ballots and observe contracts and sell goods, as well as keep Sundays. This is called dabbling with things that do not concern religion. Men say they want their blessed Sabbaths for rest and calm. They hear enough and see enough of the sins of trade during trade's six days of push and stir and strife and hot competitions and sharp bargains. "Sunday is our time for devotion," it is said. "Keep it sacred to this single use. Make us forget the world. Preach piety, nothing but piety, a beautiful, orthodox, and thoroughly respectable piety. Let us have peaceful meditations and the holy sacraments. Let us hear of nothing but sweetness and light. We don't want our Sabbaths secularized."

And alas! there have been commissioned ambassadors of the most High God, who have been

CHRISTIANITY AND BUSINESS. 241

ready to come to an agreement with this delusion, and to accept terms by which religion is relegated to one day in the week, and even then made a soothing lullaby rather than a call to righteousness; an affair of dress parade, rather than a downright service for God. The compromiser in the pulpit prays, " Thy kingdom come, Thy will be done," and the compromisers in the pews respond "Amen." But the amen even to that prayer is only meant for Sunday by these tithers of mint, anise and cummin. " Thy will be done, amen, so be it, " down through the week! Is that what the men mean who believe in this divorce of business and religion? They mean no such thing. Christianity is thought to have nothing to do with the store, the office, the counting-room and the safe investments. And the " amen " to the will of God is not intended for these secularities. What a crash it would make in some business houses, what an alteration in balance sheets, what a change in investments from where fat dividends are the order, to where only the Lord is security, if " thy will be done " were sent clean down through every avenue of trade!

We are by no means all guilty of this utter divorce of Christianity from business, or from secular affairs; from the life that occupies us through the week; but we all lean too much that way. We

16

speak of religious duties, of divine service, as if
every duty were not a religious duty, as if all service were not to be truly service for God! We do
not serve God so much by singing him psalms, as
by doing justly, and loving mercy, and walking
humbly. All duties are religious duties. There
are duties of worship and duties of work, duties of
the Sabbath, and duties of the week, duties of the
sanctuary, the closet, the counter, the mart—and
they are alike religious. True religion demands
them, if they ought to be done. Pure religion and
undefiled before God, is the doing these very things.
Divine service is rendered as much by honesty in
trade and diligence in business, as by fervency in
spirit and fidelity in prayer. The proof of piety
is not how many times you have prayed, but what
your praying has done for you; not how often
you have appeared in the pew of a Christian
Church, but how much of what you have heard in
the Church has gotten translation into action.

> " 'Tis not the wide phylactery
>   Nor stubborn fast, or stated prayers
> That make us saints. We judge the tree
>   By what it bears.
>
> "And when a man can live apart
>   From works, on theologic trust,
> I know the blood about his heart
>   Is dry as dust. "

Clearly, it is no place for Christianity alongside of business—outside of it. The right adjustment is not that of divorce or separation.

3. But the exact relation of Christianity to business is not stated, when it is said that Christianity *is to secure the righting of all wrong procedure*, or the strictest *moral rectitude*, in the transactions of men, one with another. This would be a great step indeed. This would be going down into the week with some purpose. To stop all illicit bargainings, all overreaching in trade, all misrepresentation in barter or exchange, all lying, whether by speech or by silence, all attempts at making the worse appear the better reason, all fraud from false balances or short weights, or semblance without reality, all sharp practice, everything that would not be justified at the bar of the best ethics—this would be to revolutionize trade, and change the rule of conduct of many a man who now goes unquestioned as to his business standing.

And the man who is not allowing his Christianity to do this much for him, has no Christianity worth speaking of. It matters little how he says his prayers, if he is grinding the face of the poor. The piety that keeps the Sabbath with a great zeal of devotion, yet fails to keep its possessor honest on Monday, is not the kind that is stamped in the mint

of heaven. No amount of direct effort in the behalf of the Church and of Christ, no extent of liberality, and no exhibition of the spirit of self-sacrifice
to promote spiritual ends, can ever atone for conscious and continued deflections from the path of
strict rectitude in business. The man who accus-
toms himself to take advantage of another for the
furtherance of his own interests, however such a
course may be justified in the loose maxims of a
worldly morality, will never get vindication at the
court of heaven. This much is clear. Christianity
does demand in all transactions of trade, in all professional engagements, in all financial schemes and
ventures the strictest integrity. If it does not pre-
side sovereignly over the business and worldly
work of a man to this extent, so that he is quit of
all blame by conscience and the word of God, then
that man has no right whatever to the title of Christian. The Christianity is worthless that does not
bar out of a man's secular affairs, falsehood and
personal greed and sharp practice. The Christianity is worthless that is not good behind the
counter; that will not spurn a bribe; that dare not
be overheard in the private office; that degrades
commercial transaction by low cunning, or legal
transaction by chicanery; that lies by silence; that
sells goods for more than they are known to be

worth, yet puts those same goods far below their fair value, when making returns for assessment.   I have heard men, Christian men professedly, laugh at some of these things, applaud them, hold them up as brilliant exhibitions of shrewd business diplomacy. Then I have thought of the fifteenth Psalm, which says they only shall abide in the Lord's tabernacle and dwell in his holy hill, who walk uprightly and work righteousness and speak the truth in their hearts, who put not out their money to usury, nor take reward against the innocent, nor do evil in any way to their neighbor, and it has seemed to me that these justifiers and practicers of such questionable proceedings in business, had very poor chances of getting a dwelling place in God's holy hill.   There must be pure morality in our work, or there can be no true religion in our worship. Morality is not religion, but there can be no religion without morality. The sincerely pious heart; in addition to its trust in Christ and attention to devotional duties, will aim at the highest probity and uprightness in all affairs pertaining to men.

4. But Christianity goes farther than this in its relation to business. Men may go thus far without Christianity. They do. There are noble examples of fairest morality—illustrations of honor and fidelity and virtue, that have been given without the

grace of God. A man may be beyond the reach of a bribe, honest, upright, unbreakable, true as steel, and not be a Christian. Christianity lifts a man above this level—demands this, but gives more. Truly embraced, its right relation to business is realized, only when business is done to *the glory of God.* Here we reach the high gospel ground where whatsoever we do in word or deed, we do *all* in the name of the Lord Jesus, giving God thanks. To make it impossible for us to narrow the application of this principle to so-called religious duties, the word of God carries it into the common every day necessities of life, demanding that we eat and drink to the glory of God. From these two familiar things it spreads out into everything that is lawful in life. When Christ gets into a man's heart, he is revolutionized at the seat of his moral determinations. Self ceases to be the centre. God is the spring of all his actions. Christianity has only done its appropriate work, when it has so exalted all his motives, that every labor of his hands, every transaction in trade, every professional engagement, all that relates to his temporal life, is done to the glory of God. Not that he always thinks directly and consciously of the glory of God before he enters upon any secular work—not that he distinctly says to himself before engaging in any act of business, " I do this in the name of the Lord Jesus;" but that the supreme, controlling, underlying motive of all his life is comprehended in this.

You see, now, how diligence in business may be a means of grace. Earnestness in a lawful calling—good men sometimes call it worldliness. It is not that, if the man's Christianity is making him earnest. If that go with him into his toil, inspiring him with exalted motive, he cannot fail to be earnest. And instead of his business being a hindrance to his piety, he will find it a help, and as good as prayer. .For to work in one's appointed sphere, and with right motive, is to be religious, to do a religious thing—as religious as to pray.

Understand me, I do not disparage devotional duties. They are vital. God help the man who does not take time to enter his closet and shut to his door. And if we did not have these rest and worship days we call our Sabbaths, we should be swept utterly away from our moorings, out upon a sea of worldliness. But we are in this world, citizens of it, sharers of its duties, compelled to take hold of its daily work. And after all allowances are made for other elements, it is work that rears monuments, that builds nations, that wins battles, that achieves political victories, that carries causes

of any kind anywhere. Genius is a good thing—
but industry is a better thing. The plodders in the
end are the men of achievement. The Church
is not a sponge. Christians are not pensioners.
Piety is not a sentiment. Life is a battle. Religion is business. And a first-rate Christian need
not be a fifth-rate man of business. Christianity
says, " Whatsoever thy hands find to do that is
lawful to be done, do it with the whole heart.
But do it to the glory of God! Be unworldly at
your world's work. Let not the present and the
earthly absorb you. Hold all things as not your
own. Take them and use them, and be the master
of them, not their slave." Christianity prescribes
no law for dress, for amount of business, for extent
of possessions. It establishes the great principle
of unworldliness, enjoins the being unenslaved by
earthly things, saying, Let them that buy be as
though they possessd not; i. e., so possessing that
the loss of the things possessed, shall not be like
taking away one's all; but shall leave the soul
calm, free, cheerful, master of itself, and content by
the grace of God. Buying, possessing, accumulating—this is not worldliness. But doing this in
the love of it, with no love of God paramount—doing it so that thoughts of eternity and of God are
an intrusion, deemed as having no business with

the business; doing it so that one's spirit is *secularized* in the process; this *is* worldliness. Let a man beware of this. It will eat out his piety as inevitably as he lives and allows it. Nay, to allow it, is to prove the want of piety. Get rich, if you will. You take great risks. But Christianity does not say to any man, " You must be worth only so much, extend your business only so far." It says, "Use your riches for the glory of God;" i. e., let them set loosely outside of you, while the Christ is inside regnant and worshipped. If they once usurp his place, woe to you! And you can tell whether they have your Lord's place, or not. Any man can know whether he is holding his wealth and using it to the glory of God. Any man can easily decide whether his business is being done in the name of the Lord Jesus. If it unfit him for devotion, keep him out of his closet, leave him no time for prayer, thrust itself into his hours of worship; if it secularize him, so that his religion becomes to him *intrusive* whenever it peers in at the store, the office, the shop, the counting room on a week day, and he show the door to it with a "Begone! Away with you! You belong to Sunday;" if it burden him with cares and anxieties; if it make him hard, grasping, close-fisted, ruluctant at outgoes and eager for incomes, quick for further investments in stocks and estates, but slow and doubtful about investments where the Lord is security—then Christianity has little to do with the business, and little to do with him. If he enlarge his business by contracting his religion, and swell his income by starving his soul, the balance sheet will be wofully against him in the final reckoning.

But a means of grace, a promoter of godliness, is that business done in the name of Jesus, in the spirit of consecration, its gains made useful in a Christ-like way, its ventures all baptized in prayer, its extension sought only as a means to greater good, its whole conduct and character and profit decided by considerations pertaining to the next world as well as to this. Seest thou a man diligent in such business?   He shall stand before the King.

XI.

CHRISTIANITY AND WOMAN.

From henceforth all generations shall call me blessed.
For he that is mighty hath done to me great things.
—Magnificat of THE VIRGIN.

I am prescient by the very hope
And promise set upon me, that henceforth
Only my gentleness shall make me great,
My humbleness exalt me.
—EVE, in MRS. BROWNING'S *"Drama of Exile."*

Favor is deceitful and beauty is vain; but a woman that feareth the Lord, she shall be praised.—THE PROVERBS.

CHRISTIANITY AND WOMAN.

Up in the hill country, under a Judaean sky, a Jewish maiden, standing in the mystery of a marvelous motherhood, flowered on the instant into poet and prophet. It was Mary of Nazareth, in the language of expectant faith, singing for very joy what has since been known as "the Magnificat of the Virgin."

"My soul doth magnify the Lord, and my spirit hath rejoiced in God, my Savior. For he hath regarded the low estate of his handmaiden; for, behold, from henceforth all generations shall call me blessed. For he that is mighty hath done to me great things: and holy is his name."

What a contrast between this song of the Virgin and the lament of Eve! Inspiration has not given us Eve's lament; but a gifted woman has sought to gather it out of that far silence. She thus interprets Eve's anguished heart after the sin and the curse:

"Was I not
At that last sunset seen in Paradise,

253

Mistress of feast and favor?   Could I touch
A rose with my white hand, but it became
Redder at once?   Could I walk leisurely
Along our swarded garden, but the grass
Tracked me with greenness?

Alas me! alas,
Who have undone myself from all that best,
Fairest and sweetest, to this wretchedest,
Saddest and most defiled . . For I, who lived
Beneath the wings of angels yesterday,
Wander to-day beneath a roofless world."

This is poetic conception.   But recall that first
mother, kneeling beside her murdered son—murdered by another son, and looking thus upon the
visible fruit of her sin in Paradise, and think how
the anguish must have pierced her soul!   Surely
she could never have borne it, had not hope grown
in her heart through God's blessed promise—the
hope that she, the woman, having been an Eve to
man, in God's good time, would be a Mary to him,
and give him a Savior.

God gave her a child and named it Jesus.   The
Savior of the world was born in her.   It was a
re-crowning of woman's discrowned nature, that
gift of God.   It was honoring woman with sovereign dignities.   Ever since that hour it has been
woman's heavenliest privilege to have the miracle
of the incarnation renewed in the inward history

of her heart. Ever since that hour it has been woman's one high mission to right the original wrong of Eden, and with Christ born in her own heart, to find and give him room in the great heart of the world. And ever since that hour woman's truest fame has been this—not that the world should call her beautiful, brilliant, fashionable, but *blessed.* That she has fully entered into her royal privilege, and wholly discharged her high mission, and coveted earnestly this noblest fame, cannot be said. Some have done it, thank God! Some have done it. But not woman as such, ruling in society, leading in fashion, queening in domestic life. She has too often failed of achieving her beneficent mission and of winning her peculiar glory and crown.

Yet hers is the privilege and the power through Christianity and Christ. She stands somehow related to Jesus as man does not. Mary, folded about in that mystery of motherhood, makes it impossible that there should be anything on earth more wholly in sympathy with Jesus Christ than the heart of a true Christian woman. She has even natural adaptation this way. The love that gives and the love that suffers, this is the natural love of woman. There is a love that delights itself rather in the sacrifices it *obtains,* but this is less woman's than man's. The giving, suffering, self-denying love is less man's than woman's. We know such love, we have seen it—a mother's love whose first christening, in that sorrow of sorrows reserved to her sex, is a baptism of suffering—and whose wearying, wearing watchfulness through all the subsequent days and nights of toil and care, is never broken and never ended, even though pierced and stung with what is "sharper than a serpent's tooth, a thankless child." And a wife's love, deathlessly flinging itself in a husband's descending path of disgrace and infamy to stay him from ruin, and giving her the courage for martyrdom rather than that he should go unattended and unloved.

Such love, so self-forgetful, finding joy in the sacrifices it makes, esteeming it more blessed to give than to receive, is it not oftenest born in the heart of woman? And does not this very fact make it clear that the heart of woman is more accessible to piety, and more open to the approaches of Him who by suffering conquers, and whose cross and passion give to His gospel its chief attractive power?

Then, too, the Church of Christ, beautified, purified, glorified, without spot or wrinkle or any such thing—what is it as portrayed in the Word of God, but woman, the bride of Christ, who is her

Maker and Savior, and Husband forever! Thus in divine figure is womanhood honored by Him who was born of a woman.

And how Christianity has uplifted and ennobled her, and done to her "great things," making the wo_man in whose heart Christ is born, not only the best of women, but most truly a woman, so mighty in her gentleness, so exalted in her humility, so crowned and wedded in her self-surrender.

Christianity has done this by its doctrine of equality, and by its honor of the passive virtues.

1. *By its doctrine of equality.* The gospel is a grand emancipator. It thunders against all wrong and seeks to break down every strong-hold of oppression. But mightier than its thunders is its love, melting weapons of war into implements of husbandry, lifting from bondage into freedom, transforming the spirit of tyranny into tender and trustful regard, and blotting out all iniquitous distinctions of race or sex or caste or color. From this point of view "there is neither Jew nor Greek, there is neither bond nor free, there is neither male nor female;" for all are one in Christ Jesus. It was a new gospel, this, as it came to the world eighteen centuries ago. It struck everywhere against established and throned iniquities. It broke down the middle wall of partition between Jew and Gentile,

17

and proclaimed salvation, not for Israel alone, but for the hitherto despised nations round about, deemed up to that hour aliens and ·outcasts. It broke the manacles off the limbs of bondmen, banishing slavery from the Roman Empire in three centuries; for it put the slave and his master on a level before God, made them of one blood, charged them with the same condemnation, and rendered salvation possible to them only by the same penitence, at the same altars, through the same sacrifice. It raised woman, too, from her deep degradation and doom of unpitied ignorance and toil. There is neither male nor female in Christ Jesus, i. e., neither the one nor the other has any advantage, or is entitled to any favor before God. In regard to salvation, in all that pertains to eternal life, they are on a level. They are equally precious in the sight of heaven. They are equally favored with respect to the gifts and graces of godliness. What God thus honored, what Christianity thus enriched and crowned, men could not well continue to hold in degraded position, and to treat with undisguised assumption of superiority as common and inferior.

The women of Christendom can hardly appreciate how they have been elevated by this gospel doctrine of equality. Everywhere, but in connection with Christianity, woman has been degraded, and is to-day. She has been kept in ignorance, she has been the toiler in the field, she has been secluded from society; often the mere instrument of lust; often a mere beast of burden, oppressed and enslaved at her toil; always the unhonored, uneducated, undeveloped; never the intelligent and trusted companion and friend. So is she now in China and India, and Africa, and the isles of the sea, save where Christianity has reached with its pervasive power of love and spirit of brotherhood. There she is changing into woman, the queen of home, beloved and honored as a wife and mother, at the same communion table and the same cross with the man, the intelligent sharer of his joys and griefs, his hopes and disappointments, diffusing a mild and purifying and elevating influence over all the relations of life. "Thy twain shall be one flesh." "Husbands love your wives even as Christ also loved the Church, and gave Himself for it." "Dwell with them according to knowledge, giving honor unto the wife, as being heirs together of the grace of life." "The woman is the glory of the man." "There is neither male nor female in Christ Jesus." Where precepts like these prevail, woman's degradation is impossible. They place her neither beneath nor above man, but by the side of him, in the appointment of God; neither inferior nor superior, but different—man's other self, the complement and fullness of his being. Thus Christianity uplifts and honors womanhood, links it with manhood in all holy and beneficent ministry, and makes woman more truly womanly, as she makes room for its gift of God.

But Christianity has done for woman great things, secondly:

2. By *its honor of the passive virtues*; meekness, gentleness, forbearance, forgiveness, lowliness, purity, unambitious love. Here Christianity made issue with the whole world. Before Christ was born these qualities had low place in the world's estimation. Might was deemed to consist in mere naked force, not in gentleness. Power was placed before purity; intellect before heart; strength of will before strength of affection. The qualities honored as divine were courage, wisdom, justice, strength, and these are peculiarly the qualities of the man. It was manly strength, manly justice, manly courage, manly wisdom that received divine honors and made mortals kin to the gods.

Christ came saying, Blessed are the meek, blessed are the merciful, blessed are the pure in heart, blessed are the poor in spirit, blessed are they who are persecuted for righteousness sake, resist not evil, love your enemies, bless them that curse you, do good to and pray for them that hate you. And for what grand reason did he say this? "That ye may be the children of your Father which is in heaven." As if character were to be consummated and crowned and made godlike only by the very opposite qualities from those which had hitherto had the applause and honor of the world. And are not these qualities—meekness, pureness, lovingness, patience, the passive strength of martyrdom, peculiarly the qualities of woman? Are they not distinctively feminine? Yet they are given a divine glory in the gospel of the Son of God. Those possessing them get the heavenliest benediction. They are unfolded in Christ's life, as well as honored in his speech. He is not only the one altogether mighty, but, and chiefly, the one altogether lovely. In Him, no wisdom overtops love. We never forget his gentleness in His grandest displays of power. His exaltation is His humility. "He was obedient unto death, even the death of the cross; wherefore God also hath highly exalted Him."

This is the peculiar feature of Christianity. It has no glory for the strong, no honor for the wise, but it speaks beatitudes for the patient and the meek. It makes lovingness rather than mightiness the crowning excellency. It inculcates "the idea of the divineness of what is pure, above the divineness of what is strong."

It is thus that He, who was born of Mary, hath done great things for woman. He has put exceeding honor on the passive virtues. He has shed a splendor from heaven on the order of graces that are peculiarly feminine. He has made most godlike the patience and sufferance and holy martyrdom of love, the crown-jewel in the cluster of gems making up the diadem of woman. He has lifted woman to new place in the world. And just in proportion as Christianity has sway, will she rise to a higher dignity in human life. What she has now, and what she shall have, of privilege and true honor, she owes to that gospel which took those qualities peculiarly her own and which had been counted weak and unworthy, and gave them a divine glory in Christ. Jesus cannot conquer a place in the world by his gentleness and patience and suffering love, without commanding for the divineness of purity, and the exaltation of humility, and the strength of obedience, their right and deserved acknowledgment. And just as this is done will woman's place be higher, and her influence broader, and the number greater who shall call her blessed.

Yes, "blessed!" That is the word. It is woman's truest fame. It was Mary's crown—her glory— her satisfying, blissful joy. They have mocked the lowly Virgin with such homage since, they have lifted her to such so-called dignities, they have named her with such other names, that the gentle spirit of her Hebrew song seems like a rebuke to the wicked idolatry. The Romish church has falsified Mary's word.

We may be sure that this Jewish hand-maiden in the blessedness of her blessedness bowed her heart lower than the knees of all other worshipers, and that now in heaven the very thought of wearing the titles manufactured for her by a perverting priesthood would pierce her like a shame. The only glory she won and wore on earth was the glory of true womanhood. It was not immaculate origin, nor immaculate life, nor exaltation to divine honors as queen of heaven. It was not prerogative of power or place—not force, not wisdom, not demanded rights. It was womanhood in lowliness and loveliness rejoicing in God her Savior, and content to be called blessed.

So Christianity comes to woman desiring that its Christ shall be born in her—no more indeed after the flesh, but after the spirit. This is her heavenliest privilege. Then, with sense of her in-

debtedness, Christianity bids her go forth with the
patience of love and the spirit of sacrifice, to give
this Christ to others. What higher mission and
grander work has woman than this! To be filled
with gratitude for the outward benefits of Christianity, sensible that she owes everything to this
gospel of the Son of God, to welcome to her heart
the brooding Spirit, through whose overshadowing
Christ may be born to her, and then to go forth
with Jesus in her heart on a ministry of love and
mercy, breaking her alabaster box of precious ointment for the sin-smitten and sorrow-laden, so that
they filled too with the fragrance of Jesus, may
carry her dear anointing to their burial! O for
such womanhood, unwilling simply to be lapped
in the folds of a silken and easy life, caring not to
be called fashionable, content to be called blessed—
willing to lose all thought of self, of finery and
pleasure, in an earnest effort, with a passion of love
and a patience of hope, to relieve and heal the sorrow and the vice of the world. O for such
women, ambitious not to vote, but to be—not to
make additions to political rights, but to acquire
personal and moral worth—not to have more authority and to be a power like force, but to have
more influence and to be a power like love. Is
this deemed a mission without honor and unworthy

of woman? Then unworthy was the mission of the Son of God; for this was His. He came not to be ministered unto but to minister, not to save himself but others, not to conquer and possess by the might of mere power, but by love and sacrifice.

We have such womanhood. But we have, alas, much that is anything else. "Society" is woman's expression of certain ideas, for society is measurably under her control. We have women ambitious to queen it there, even at the expense of their children and their souls; whose idea of hospitality is an unlimited table, an exhibition of plate and furniture, and a round of airy nothings and dreary emptiness of talk; whose idea of marriage is, not that it is the most solemn of all contracts between two human souls, of which God is the perpetual witness and judge, but instead, a sham show for the benefit of the public, parading one day as millionaires, even though to sink back to debt and obscurity the next; whose idea of home is, not a sphere of order and love and law, hallowed and peaceful, but a place of living, a base of supplies, a dry-dock for repairs, a peg on which to hang the appearance, if not the reality, of wealth.

Thus have these solemn verities, hospitality, marriage, home, entrusted to woman's keeping, been belittled and degraded by, alas! too many who have claimed to be leaders in society. And their perversion of these sanctities of life has had its baneful influence down through all the different social levels, making women there, according to the measure of their means, the same delighters in gew-gaws and the same paraders of shams.

O, that woman would end all this, and exalt womanhood, by being true to herself! She has a great work to do—a mighty work; and before her just now God sets an open door. Within her reach are possibilities of influence unbounded. Of all the forces, physical, mental, and moral, the moral are the mightiest; and art and poetry in all the Christian ages have personified the moral powers by woman. Christianity is lifting these to higher and higher place. The world is destined yet to think far more of love and patience and gentleness, and the suffering spirit of sacrifice; and far less relatively of authority and force and the might to win bloody battles. The courage to endure shall be prized increasingly above the courage to fight. The laureled and trumpeted winners of victories, the world's garlanded heroes, shall yet be those who conquer by deeds of faith and generous ministry; by love that asks not, but gives and suffers; by deathless patience—the outreaching and self-denying of womanly hearts, daring to be singular rather than be untrue.

I stand amazed before the revelations of the last decade of years as to how a woman may help Christ's Kingdom come. What unused and un-guessed resources have been lying hid, that this "woman's work for woman" has called out of their secret places, and sent on missionary errands around the world! It is the dawn of a new day—and there scarcely has been a brighter since the angels made the Judaean air thick with melody when Jesus was born. It looks, after all, as if the strategic point in the warfare for this world's su-premacy were the heart of woman. That won, and the family is won. And when "up goes the family, down goes heathenism."

To secure a change of levels like this, to bring about the uplifting of womanly hearts, woman surely has peculiar adaptations. In this business there are paths where her feet are already shown to be the swiftest; needs, she by all odds is the fittest to meet; ministries, it has already been her abysmal joy to share. For this business the Mar-thas and Marys, the Tryphenas and Tryphosas, the Phoebes and Dorcases, must be multiplied as the drops of the morning.

The world waits for such women. The field opens. The hour strikes. Women of America, "beneath the cross or never!" There only can you

be truly crowned and wedded. First, your hearts
to Christ.   Then, Christ born in them, and a constant dweller there.   Then, forth upon your mission to find room for the gift of God in the great
heart of the world.   You can do nothing! You
can do everything.   You can *give* and *serve* and
pray. You can give self-denyingly. You can
serve lovingly. You can pray conqueringly. The
best example of self-denying liberality in the Bible
is recorded of woman. The best example of loving service in the Bible is recorded of woman.
The best example of conquering prayer in the
Bible is recorded of woman. It was no great gift,
no great service, no great prayer. The gift was a
widow's mite. The service was the anointing of
Jesus with a box of ointment. The prayer was a
mother's prayer for a daughter possessed with a
devil.   But the gift and service and prayer were
in self-denial and love and faith.   And so in the
sight of God they were of great price. Jesus never
let fall such words of royal commendation as concerning these three women.   Of the poor widow
he said, "She hath cast in more than they all." Of
Mary with her alabaster box of precious ointment
he said, "She hath done what she could."   And to
the praying Canaanitish mother he said, "O woman,
great is thy faith. Be it unto thee even as thou
wilt." The human suppliant had power with

God, and the Creator said to the creature, "Thy
will be done." Surely such giving, such service,
such prayer is possible to every woman. It is not
the greatness of it, but the spirit of it, that tells. O
ye women, whether of affluence or poverty, whether of high place or low place, whether old or young,
go at the call of Christianity and do your woman's
work. There are treasuries of the Lord that wait
your mites. There are alabaster boxes you may
break for Jesus, if not upon Him. There are
daughters, O how many, this wide world over, in
Christendom and heathendom with evil possessions, whom you by faith may bring to Christ for
healing

　　　　　　"Henceforward, rise to all
The sanctified devotion and full work
To which thou art elect forevermore."

　　　　　　"Rise
To thy peculiar and best altitudes
Of doing good and of enduring ill."

　　　　　　"If wo by thee
Had issue to the world, thou shalt go forth
An angel of the wo thou didst achieve."

　　　　　　"A child's kiss
Set on thy lips shall make thee glad:
A poor man served by thee shall make thee rich—
A sick man helped by thee shall make thee strong;
Thou shalt be served thyself by every sense
Of service which thou renderest."

CUSHING, THOMAS AND COMPANY, PUBLISHERS.

Calendora and Other Poems.

By JAMES H. SCOTT.

——(Will be published in May, 1881.)——

One Volume, 16mo.   Price, $1.00.

THE MAIDEN'S PRAYER.

When loud the billows roar,
And strew the shore
With broken spars,
And I
Decry
Beneath the stars
Nor sail, nor oar,
For thee my prayer I pour.

When upward to the sky
My weary eye
Unconscious turns
In prayer,
E'en there
My faith discerns
Thy spirit nigh,
And whispers, "By-and-By."

Rocked on the briny deep,
Soft be thy sleep,
And sweet thy dreams
My love.
Above
Play gentle beams,
And angels keep
My chosen, on the deep.

Sold by Booksellers, or mailed post-paid, on receipt of price by
CUSHING, THOMAS & CO., Publishers, CHICAGO.

www.ingramcontent.com/pod-product-compliance
Lightning Source LLC
Chambersburg PA
CBHW021059030726
47496CB00006B/1918